"In the better days that lie ahead,
men will speak with pride of our doings."
— General Bernard Montgomery

DAN VAN DER VAT   Introduction by JOHN S. D. EISENHOWER

D-DAY

THE GREATEST INVASION — A PEOPLE'S HISTORY

BLACK WALNUT

A BLACK WALNUT BOOKS

This book is dedicated to the Canadian soldiers who landed in Normandy in
June 1944 and liberated my hometown, Alkmaar in North Holland, in May 1945.

— Dan van der Vat

Jacket, design, and compilation © 2003 The Madison Press Limited
Text © 2003 Dan van der Vat
Introduction © 2003 John S.D. Eisenhower
Photographs by Peter Christopher © 2003

This edition published in 2007 by
Black Walnut Books,
an imprint of Madison Press Books.

ISBN-13: 978-1-897330-27-2
ISBN-10: 1-897330-27-8

For more information, please contact

Black Walnut Books
c/o Madison Press Books
1000 Yonge Street, Suite 200
Toronto, Ontario
Canada M4W 2K2

Printed in China

(Page 1) A Canadian
invasion-pattern helmet
beside operational orders.
(Pages 2–3) Omaha Beach
today. (Inset) U.S. assault
troops in a landing craft
approach a beachhead
on June 6, 1944.
(Right) Inside a surviving
gun emplacement atop
Pointe du Hoc overlooking
Omaha Beach.

(Left) American glider pilots leave Normandy after successfully landing soldiers in France. (Right) Identification "dog tags" issued to U.S. troops.

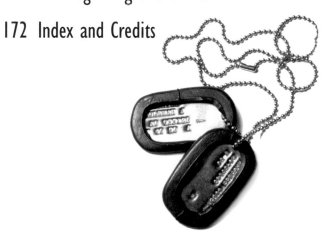

by John S. D. Eisenhower

(Above) John Eisenhower, right, with his father in 1945.

■ "OKAY, WE'LL GO." With that simple, homely sentence, General Dwight D. Eisenhower, Supreme Commander, Allied Expeditionary Force, launched Operation Overlord — the long-awaited invasion of Western Europe in the Second World War. These words were uttered in the early morning hours of June 5, 1944. The next day, June 6, would become famous in history as "D-Day."

Once that order was given, the mightiest amphibious invasion force in history began cutting its way through the waters around the United Kingdom — an armada of 5,000 ships carrying 130,000 men and 20,000 vehicles, supported by the gunfire of 700 warships, including six monstrous battleships. Eight thousand aircraft were involved. All these were to converge at first light along a stretch of Norman beach from the Cotentin Peninsula on the west to Caen on the east — a distance of fifty miles. Five beaches had been selected for the landings; two were to be taken by the Americans, one by the Canadians, and two by the British. To protect the flanks of the assaulting troops, three airborne divisions — two American and one British — were to drop in the early morning, a couple of hours before the seaborne troops would come ashore.

The stakes in the venture were enormous. The Allies — the Americans, British and Canadians — were literally putting all their eggs in one basket. The invasion of Nazi-held Western Europe had been their objective from the very first days of America's entry into the war. Through two and a half years of grim warfare, the Allies never lost sight of their ultimate goal: the defeat of Hitler's Germany by means of a massive assault through France. Nobody underestimated its importance. Success would mean the liberation of enslaved Western Europe; failure would result in a stalemate, possibly of years. Or, if the German forces facing the Russians collapsed, it would mean an occupation of Western Europe by Joseph Stalin's Soviet Union. Neither situation could be tolerated. Overlord had to succeed.

By the spring of 1944, the fact that the Allies were planning an assault across the English Channel was no secret. American troops had been pouring into the United Kingdom for months, and their presence was being felt all too keenly by the British populace. Vast stores of supplies not only filled the warehouses but lined the roadsides as well. The names of the top Allied generals and admirals were publicly announced. There were only two secrets to the invasion: when it would come and where it would occur.

German intelligence knew when the day came near. The atmosphere in May 1944 was electric all over England and Scotland; the whole of southern England was sealed off from communication with the outside world. On the question of where, however, the Germans had less to go on. Their guess, quite logically, was that the Allies would cross the English Channel at the Pas de Calais. The English Channel is only twenty-one miles wide at that point, and the Pas de Calais is three hundred miles closer to Germany than the other possible landing area, Normandy. Even though Hitler gave his priority to Calais, the German defenses of Normandy were strong and growing. Hitler's most high-profile general, Field Marshal Erwin Rommel, had been placed in charge of preparing those defenses, and his photograph, taken while he was inspecting the great gun emplacements, reached the American and British publics. No one doubted that, wherever the landings occurred, the going would be tough.

Everyone waited in suspense on both sides of the Atlantic. And, as with other cataclysmic events, those who experienced early June 1944 still remember where they were when the news first arrived. That is particularly so in my case. By the most extraordinary coincidence, I graduated from West Point as a member of the Class of 1944 on that date. Despite the war, West Point had gone through its usual week-long series of graduation rituals — ceremonies, parades and formal dances. On the morning of June 6, 1944, as the Corps of Cadets fell into ranks to march to breakfast, I took my customary place as first battalion sergeant major behind Cadet Battalion Commander Alan Weston. Weston turned and looked at me quizzically: "You've heard, I guess, that the Allies landed in Normandy this morning." I had not.

Americans received this news with a mixture of relief and apprehension. It was good to know that the Allies were ashore, but would they be able to stay? For my part, as the son of the supreme commander, General Eisenhower, I felt a special apprehension. I was not so concerned for the inevitable risk to my father's career — the stakes were much too high to worry about that — but in common with families of other prominent people, I felt a share of responsibility for the enterprise. During that whole day, the landing in Normandy was never out of my mind as West Point went through with its program.

Finally, the ceremonies were over. The banks of newspaper photographers left, and I joined my mother in the Thayer Hotel to change uniforms. My classmates were going on a month's leave, but I was headed for the New York Port of Embarkation to board the *Queen Mary*, the British liner that had been converted into a troop carrier. General George C. Marshall had ordered me to spend about three weeks with my father in London, after which I would return and join my classmates at the Infantry School. The *Queen Mary* sailed that very evening. I would have to endure a full week without word as to how the landings had gone.

In London I found my father restless but cheerful. He had recovered from the strain of his agonizing decision a week earlier to launch the invasion despite the miserable weather conditions. He was not one to look back, and he said little about that decision. He did, however, mention one aspect with a wry grin. "On the morning that I decided to postpone the invasion, the weather was beautiful.

The stars were out and the air was warm. The next morning, when we would have gone, the rain was coming down in torrents, almost horizontal. But acceptable weather was predicted for June 6, so I decided to go. At least the rains assured me that the meteorologists had some idea of what they were doing." Then he shrugged and his mind turned to other business.

In the days that followed, I accompanied my father twice to Normandy and once to call on Prime Minister Winston Churchill. The most memorable day, however, was June 19, 1944, when a storm hit the English Channel, the most virulent in fifty years. Had General Eisenhower delayed the invasion of Normandy pending the next date of favorable tide and moon conditions, he would have faced this storm. It seemed almost eerie to both of us, a matter of Providence perhaps.

Over the passage of sixty years, the memories of these personal matters fade. What remains in our consciousness is what should remain — the heroism of the men who actually hit the beaches. For they were the ones to whom the triumph of D-Day belongs. All the planning, the transport of supplies, the training and even the order to go were mere directions to the central figures of D-Day — the members of the assault divisions. I have felt a secret discomfort that West Point's Class of 1944 was savoring its graduation at the same time that boys younger than us were clinging desperately to the cliffs of Normandy or sinking in the English Channel, and yet finally pulling themselves together to launch the beginning of the liberation of Europe. It is a humbling thought.

THIS BOOK, *D-DAY: THE GREATEST INVASION*, IS A TRIBUTE TO ALL THE veterans of Normandy. While it provides background for the invasion and gives proper recognition to the planners and commanders, it recognizes that the everyday soldier really occupies center stage. It tells us of the heroes of Pegasus Bridge, of the Canadians at Juno Beach and of the American 1st Division, with the 116th Infantry, at Omaha Beach. Those men, and many others, are the heroes of this book. It is an honor to join in paying this tribute — especially because the year 2004 will represent the last ten-year anniversary of D-Day for nearly all of them.

— *John S. D. Eisenhower, Eastern Shore, Maryland, April 2003*

So Much Was at Stake

■ IN ALKMAAR, A MARKET TOWN in the Dutch province of North Holland, the news of the Allied landing in France on June 6, 1944, evoked a mixture of euphoria and apprehension — as it did all over Nazi-occupied Europe. I was born there in 1939, to an English mother and a Dutch father, and lived there until the end of 1945. My first memories are of the German occupation of the town — and of our liberation by the Canadian army at the very end of the Second World War.

So, assuming their landing succeeded, the Allies were coming at last. But how much death and destruction would the defeat of Hitler add to the four years of suffering and fear already endured? This anxiety would prove particularly well-founded in all of the Netherlands north of the Rhine, which was bypassed in the Allied drive toward the Ruhr and Berlin. We were thus not liberated until the bitter end of the war in Europe, by the Canadians. By then many thousands of Dutch people had needlessly and tragically died of starvation in the notorious "Hunger Winter."

This personal reminiscence is offered as one small example of how much was at stake on the broad, sandy beaches of Normandy on what went down in history as "D-Day." My vivid recollection of the end of the Second World War in Holland is one reason why I wrote this book.

Although it was a serious offense to listen to the BBC, my parents — like many others — regularly tuned in on an illegal crystal wireless set they had hidden up the living-room chimney. (Since we did not have any fuel, there was no better use for the chimney.) We lived directly opposite a youth camp turned German barracks, and the house next door was under military occupation, so the risk was not to be taken lightly. At midday on June 6, the BBC announced:

Under the command of General Eisenhower, Allied naval forces supported by strong air forces began landing Allied armies this morning on the coast of France.

There are other reasons for this re-examination of D-Day and the ensuing struggle for victory in Normandy. I met many veterans of the campaign when I visited the area during my research. There were hearteningly large numbers of elderly ex-soldiers in their blazers, berets and medals. More than a few relied on wheelchairs, crutches or canes, but the majority seemed in good spirits — thanks in large measure to the hospitality of the people of Normandy, repeated every June. But it is a sobering thought, as the sixtieth anniversary looms, that a soldier who was just eighteen years old on June 6, 1944, is approaching his seventy-eighth year now. Many of the veterans I met were considerably older; several veterans' associations have already disbanded for lack of numbers. The sixtieth is therefore especially poignant as the last "round number" anniversary likely to be attended by a notable number of participants in Adolf Hitler's greatest defeat.

MANY FINE BOOKS HAVE BEEN WRITTEN ABOUT D-DAY AND WHAT followed. Some are oral histories, while others concentrate on grand strategy; yet others focus on one nation's (or one individual's) role. As a veteran of sorts myself, though only of military history, I offer this all-round, warts-and-all view of the conflict — looking at it not only from both sides but also from above (the strategic aspect) and below (quoting ordinary soldiers, sailors and airmen). Such an overall perspective is not unique, but it is unusual. The purpose of the text, supported by many illustrations and explanatory material, is to offer the reader a clear overview — not only of who did what where and when, but also how and why they did it.

— *Dan van der Vat, London, April 2003*

(Opposite) Headstones in the Canadian War Cemetery at Bény-sur-Mer, Reviers, Normandy.

The Decisive Front

"The big question mark always before us was the weather...."

— General Dwight D. Eisenhower, Supreme Commander, Allied Expeditionary Force

(Opposite) Southwick House today.
(Above) General Eisenhower, right,
and Admiral Ramsay confer in front of
the portico at Southwick.

GENERAL "IKE" EISENHOWER and the admirals, generals and air marshals who would lead the imminent invasion of Hitler's "Fortress Europe" gathered for their customary after-dinner meeting on Sunday, June 4, 1944. As usual they sank into the deep armchairs of the Senior Messroom at Southwick House, an elegant Georgian mansion set in an ancient forest ten miles northwest of Portsmouth in the south of England. The estate had been the Royal Navy's School of Navigation until it was taken over by Admiral Sir Bertram Ramsay, Allied naval commander in chief, as his invasion headquarters. Since May 28, when the daily high-command meetings commenced (twice daily from June 2), it had also been Eisenhower's forward headquarters. This grand company was waiting anxiously for a relatively junior officer, Group Captain James Stagg, RAF, to make his usual modest and laconic contribution — the weather forecast.

A successful assault on the beaches of Normandy depended above all upon the weather. Not even the other great imponderable in the plan for Operation Overlord, the enemy's response, caused Eisenhower as much anxiety as the treacherous Channel. Sea conditions — the extreme tides of the new-moon period, which would enable the invaders to deal with German underwater obstacles and then be carried as close to the beaches as possible — would cease to be suitable after June 6. The next opportunity would come at full moon two weeks later, but Stagg feared that the chances of acceptable conditions would only be half as good. And an invasion after June would be too late to gain the upper hand over the Germans before winter.

As the daily briefing began, the prolonged daylight of Double Summer Time outside the multipaned windows presented a gloomy picture of cloud and squally rain. A day earlier, Stagg — a tall, lean Scot who was Eisenhower's chief meteorological adviser — had forecast five days of continuing squalls in the Channel. His prediction had persuaded a depressed Eisenhower at the dawn meeting to postpone the invasion by

(Above) War artist Barnett Freedman captured the activity in the map room on the ground floor of Southwick House, the nerve center of operations during the planning of Operation Overlord. Information on maps was updated every half hour. (Inset) The preserved map room today.

twenty-four hours. Tens of thousands of troops and sailors were thus condemned to a wretched extra day and night in a heaving sea. The enemy might be beaten by human effort, but the weather could not be — and time was running out.

When the weatherman had left the messroom on the evening of June 3, a British admiral remarked: "There goes six feet two inches of Stagg and six feet one of gloom." Lieutenant General Sir Frederick Morgan, chief planner of the invasion, had earlier teased the weatherman with a heavy hand: "Good luck, Stagg; may all your depressions be little ones. But remember we'll string you up from the nearest lamppost if you don't read the omens right...."

Yet there was still hope that an unexpected new weather front might materialize in the volatile North Atlantic. By the evening of Sunday, June 4, Group Captain Stagg believed he had found one.

AN UNSEASONAL COLD FRONT APPROACHING FROM THE ATLANTIC HAD accelerated sharply during the day but also changed direction. At the same time, the depression behind it slowed down. Stagg deduced that a relatively calm period of perhaps twenty-four hours would come between the two. This weather-window would bring only scattered clouds — although the wind and waves would be at the high end of the planners' acceptable range.

It should therefore be possible to put the first assault troops ashore on the incoming tide soon after dawn on Tuesday, and to land massive follow-up forces after the evening ebb a little over twelve hours later. Naval and air support for the landings would not be, Stagg hoped, significantly affected by the indifferent visibility expected for the night of June 5–6 and the ensuing day.

What was more, the Germans — lacking the elaborate air- and seaborne weather-reporting network set up by the North Atlantic Allies — could well be caught unawares by the lull. This would increase the chance of achieving tactical surprise — an aim to which a uniquely elaborate program of deception before, during and after the invasion was dedicated.

The tension in the silent conference room was palpable as Eisenhower and his commanders listened once again to Stagg's report. Ike then invited comments. He turned last to his army commander in chief, General Sir Bernard "Monty" Montgomery: "Do you see any reason why we should not go on Tuesday?" The slight, untidy figure who would lead the armies in France replied briskly in his famous, reedy voice: "No. I would say, Go!"

An acutely nervous Stagg was responsible for the content and pitch of his fateful advice — culled with great difficulty from sources often at odds with one another, and subsequently described as the most important weather forecast in history. But Eisenhower alone bore the unique burden of choosing whether to accept it. His decision to take the calculated risk of doing so was unsurpassed for moral courage throughout the war.

At the end of May 1944, two million troops across southern England were poised to launch and follow up on the greatest amphibious assault ever — the planned invasion of Nazi-occupied Europe that was called Operation Overlord. They were supported by about 4,000 landing craft, 3,500 amphibious vehicles, 8,000 planes and 284 major warships.

The initial assault force of five infantry divisions — preceded by massive air and sea bombardments and led by seaborne tanks — was to attack the beaches across a fifty-mile front, whose flanks to east and west were to be secured a few hours in advance by three airborne divisions dropped in the dark. The outcome would then depend chiefly on whether the Allies could reinforce faster by sea than the Germans — harried by the bombardments and by Resistance attacks — could by land.

Far on the other side of the Greater German Reich, the Russians were poised to mount a new offensive to hold down the German army on its eastern front. They had been clamoring for a second front in the west for more than a year. The peoples of occupied Europe were longing for liberation from Nazi oppression. Free fighting men from many of the oppressed countries — desperate to get home to France or Poland, Holland or Norway — were strongly represented among the forces that would follow on the heels of the invaders. So much and more depended on D-Day.

Relief — albeit a day late because of the weather — was at hand.

It All Came down to the Weather

To make his forecast, meteorologist James Stagg (below) had to balance several different, often contradictory, requirements. The transport aircraft needed a cloud ceiling of not less than 2,500 feet over their targets, and 3-mile visibility. The medium bombers also wanted 3-mile visibility — but their ceiling had to be 4,500 feet. The heavy bombers were not fussy about visibility, but wanted no more than 5/10ths cloud cover below 5,000 feet and a ceiling of 11,000 feet over their targets. For the navy, the winds were not to exceed 12 MPH onshore or 18 MPH offshore. The paratroopers could cope as long as winds didn't exceed 20 MPH and weren't gusty. The army wanted it dry enough to take heavy vehicles off the main roads.

As if this weren't bad enough, to predict these conditions Stagg had to reconcile often wildly variant forecasts. The navy might tell him one thing; the government's civilian meteorologists something else. American forecasters tended to be overly optimistic; their British counterparts excessively pessimistic. Small wonder Stagg was later to comment, "If every one of the requirements I had been given was to be insisted on, it was easy to deduce that Overlord might not get underway for another hundred years or more."

The northwest coast of Normandy today. It was along this fifty-mile stretch of wide, flat beaches that the Allies launched their massive assault against Hitler's formidable Atlantic Wall.

CHAPTER ONE

The Plan

"An operation of the nature and size of Operation Overlord has never previously been attempted in history."

— Outline of Operation Overlord (official document)

EUROPE 1944: THE EVE OF INVASION

NORWAY

Oslo

SWEDEN

BALTIC SEA

DENMARK

NORTH SEA

Copenhagen

EAST PRUSSIA

IRELAND

UNITED KINGDOM

NETHERLANDS

London

The Hague

BELGIUM

Berlin

GERMANY

Warsaw

POLAND

ATLANTIC OCEAN

Dieppe

Brussels

Prague

Paris

CZECHOSLOVAKIA

BAY OF BISCAY

FRANCE

Zurich

Vienna

SWITZERLAND

AUSTRIA

Budapest

HUNGARY

PORTUGAL

SPAIN

Madrid

ITALY

ADRIATIC SEA

YUGOSLAVIA

MEDITERRANEAN SEA

Front line, Jan 1944

Rome

ALBANIA

GREECE

Operation Husky (Invasion of Sicily, July 10, 1943)

Operation Torch (November 8, 1942)

Sep 3, 1943

Algiers

Sep 9, 1943

Sep 9, 1943

MOROCCO

Casablanca

Allied Advance

ALGERIA

Under Prime Minister Winston Churchill (below), Britain spearheaded the Allied assault that drove the Axis forces from North Africa, followed by the invasion of Sicily and Italy in 1943. Despite these defeats, however, Adolf Hitler (above) still had a firm grip on Western Europe in early 1944 (opposite).

■ THE ANGLO-AMERICAN ALLIES disagreed fundamentally on strategy for defeating the Nazis. Long before Pearl Harbor brought the United States into the conflict, Britain and the United States had agreed in principle that beating Germany would take precedence over fighting Japan. Precisely how they would do this, however, was a contentious issue.

The Americans wanted to attack the main force of the main enemy as soon as possible by invading northern France and driving toward Germany from the west while the Russians pursued their great land campaign in the east.

Britain favored a different approach. The British had been forced into a succession of retreats by an apparently insuperable Wehrmacht. Humiliation in Norway had been followed by disaster in France and the Low Countries and by ignominious routs in Greece and Crete. After the evacuation of the bulk of its expeditionary force from Dunkirk in June 1940, Britain had a disarmed rump of an army and no major ally. It faced apparently imminent invasion and had no hope of defeating the Germans unaided. Hitler's massive assault on the Soviet Union one year later may have ended the military isolation of the British Empire, but it made no immediate difference to the invincibility of German-occupied Europe — even if the Russians were soon absorbing the attention of two-thirds of the German army. The British therefore chose to fight on the fringe of Axis-held territory in the Mediterranean and North Africa, while imposing a naval blockade on German-occupied Western Europe and steadily building up the aerial bombardment of Germany itself.

The Americans regarded the British military effort of 1941–42 in North Africa and the Mediterranean as a sideshow. The U.S. chiefs of staff pressed for a limited landing in German-occupied northern France as early as summer 1942. Their idea was to help the Red Army, gathering strength but still on the defensive after the German invasion. They wanted to follow this with a full-scale invasion in spring 1943. The British regarded such ideas as dangerously premature, proposing instead a landing on the Atlantic coast of French North Africa to help Montgomery's 8th Army drive the Axis powers out of the region. Churchill put this formally to Roosevelt in spring 1942, and Operation Torch — the seaborne invasion of North Africa — was born.

The invasion of France remained on the table as a proposal with no set date. Indeed, Torch would delay such an enterprise by absorbing massive resources, including scarce landing craft. But the British showed their willingness by mounting a limited attack on a port on the eastern fringe of Normandy — Operation Jubilee, better known as the Dieppe Raid. It was an unmitigated disaster, particularly for the Canadian army, which provided the bulk of the troops that assaulted the French city on August 19, 1942. The attackers lost the element of surprise, and most of the assaulting troops found themselves pinned on the beaches. Of the 5,000 Canadian soldiers who landed (along with the Royal Marines and a few American rangers), 907 were killed and 1,874 taken prisoner.

Yet the catastrophe provided priceless lessons for a full-scale amphibious invasion. A successful landing would require first-class prior intelligence and a heavy preliminary air and naval bombardment. And it would have to be a landing on open beaches — a direct attack on a large port from the sea was out of the question. Infantry could not assault strongly defended beaches without close armored support. Further, every effort would be made to achieve tactical surprise, not easy when it was obvious to both sides that an invasion was not a matter of "if" but of "when." Perhaps most important was the recognition that such an invasion could not happen before 1944. Only then would enough men and supplies be available.

Thanks largely to meticulous planning by Admiral Ramsay, Torch went well in November 1942, just after Montgomery defeated Rommel in the decisive battle of El Alamein. The Axis powers gave up the struggle for North Africa in May 1943. Yet the British were still resisting U.S. (and Soviet) pressure for an immediate second front in northwest Europe. The balance of power in the Anglo-American alliance was by now shifting permanently to the Americans. But Prime Minister Winston Churchill got his way one last time at the summit conference with President Franklin D. Roosevelt and their senior aides in Casablanca, Morocco, in January 1943. The next undertaking would be Operation Husky, an invasion of Sicily six months later — to be followed by assaults on the Italian mainland.

Finally, in spring 1943, the Anglo-American combined chiefs of staff agreed in principle on the invasion of northwest France — Operation Overlord. And in March, Lieutenant General Morgan was appointed Chief of Staff to the Supreme Allied Commander (COSSAC) to plan the invasion — even though nobody had yet been chosen, or even nominated, for this post.

Smoke rises over Casablanca during the early days of Operation Torch — the Allied invasion of northwest Africa in November 1942. By the following May, Germany had lost the war in Africa, along with large numbers of troops, weapons and supplies.

The Costly Lesson of Dieppe

It ranks among the greatest disasters of the war in Europe. On August 19, 1942, Britain's Combined Operations Command sent 252 ships carrying some 6,100 troops and 30 tanks from southern England across the Channel to the coast of eastern Normandy to attack at dawn. Their goal was the French seaside town of Dieppe. Most of the troops were Canadians from two infantry brigades — nearly five thousand men — supported by about one thousand British commandos plus small American and Free French special-forces units.

Their objective was dangerously vague. As a "reconnaissance in force," they were to seize a major port and hold it — a move the Allies hoped would take pressure off the struggling Russians by forcing the Germans to move troops from east to west. There was no plan for a follow-up to the first assault waves. In fact, there were no reinforcements available for one.

Before the troops even landed, everything went wrong. Some of the landing craft blundered into a small German convoy. The noise of battle alerted nearby shore defenses. Now the Germans knew they were coming. When the main assault force landed at Dieppe, the men faced murderous machine-gun fire. Their few tanks landed late, and many bogged down in the shingle or were trapped by the seawall. Few Allied soldiers even got off the beach.

After nine hours of bitter fighting, the lucky few were evacuated. Allied casualties — killed, wounded, missing or captured — reached about 4,100, more than two-thirds of the total attack force. This included 907 Canadians killed and 1,874 taken

"If I had the same decision to make again, I would do as I did before. It gave the Allies the priceless secret of victory."
— Admiral Lord Mountbatten

prisoner. One destroyer and three landing craft were sunk. The Royal Navy suffered 550 casualties, including 75 killed. The RAF and RCAF lost 99 planes — the worst one-day total of the war. By contrast, 314 Germans were killed, 294 wounded and 37 captured; 48 of their aircraft were lost.

And what did the Allies gain for so much lost? The Germans did not move significant forces from east to west, but they did strengthen coastal defenses in France. Today, popular opinion holds that the bloody mistakes of Dieppe contributed to the Allied successes at Normandy — giving the Allies hard-won but much-needed lessons in how to carry out an invasion.

(Above) Canadian troops storm ashore at Dieppe on August 19, 1942, in a dramatic painting by war artist Charles Comfort. (Below, left) Wrecked equipment and bodies litter the beach in the aftermath of the failed raid. (Middle) German soldiers inspect one of the few Canadian tanks to make it off the beach. (Right) These Canadian soldiers were among the approximately two thousand Allied prisoners taken at Dieppe.

In July 1943, Morgan's planners completed their first draft — a brilliant achievement in just four months, as well as a sound foundation for eventual success. It called for an initial assault by three divisions across a thirty-mile front on the northwest coast of Normandy while airborne troops took Caen, the strategically crucial Norman capital to the south of the chosen beaches. Cherbourg, the major port at the northern end of the Cotentin Peninsula to the west, was to be taken from the landward side in fourteen days, with support from sea and air. While many more troops could be landed from the sea once the beachheads were joined up in an established bridgehead, the Allies needed large ports as early as possible for the massive supplies and reinforcements required by their drive across northern Europe to the Ruhr and Berlin.

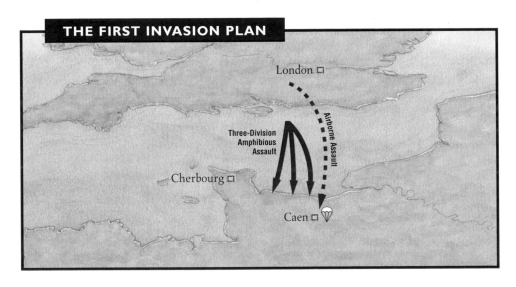

THE FIRST INVASION PLAN

London □

Three-Division
Amphibious
Assault

Airborne Assault

Cherbourg □

Caen □

The COSSAC staff realized that an assault wave of just three divisions was not enough, but they were limited by the chronic shortage of landing craft — swallowed up mainly by the Americans' island-hopping campaign in the Pacific. Nonetheless, at another summit meeting in Quebec in August 1943, Overlord was provisionally fixed for the beginning of May 1944. By that time the Anglo-American invasion of Sicily had produced a qualified success — the island was soon taken, but forty thousand German combat troops escaped to the Italian mainland with their equipment. Also, rivalry between Montgomery and American Lieutenant General George S. Patton — born of their race for Messina in northeast Sicily — laid the foundation of a dangerous personal animosity, one of many among Allied leaders that would affect the course of events in France.

The high commanders for Overlord were selected by the Anglo-American combined chiefs of staff and confirmed by Churchill and Roosevelt in December 1943. After Eisenhower's successes with Torch and Husky, his appointment as Supreme Allied Commander (SAC) looks inevitable in hindsight, but the two army chiefs of staff —

(Above, left) The Allies' first invasion plan called for a three-division amphibious attack across the English Channel to the Normandy coast. (Above, right) Seated in the center, General Eisenhower confers with General Montgomery, right, during a meeting of commanders for Operation Overlord. (Opposite) Allied headquarters were at Norfolk House, in St. James's Square.

The D-Day Commanders — Eisenhower and Montgomery

They were unlikely partners, the laconic American midwesterner and the peppery British clergyman's son, but together they commanded the Allied forces taking part in D-Day. And although they were never close, each respected the other.

Charismatic but not flashy, Dwight D. Eisenhower (above, left) was widely viewed as the ideal choice for supreme commander of the Allied invasion forces. As a cadet at West Point, he was remembered by fellow students for his natural leadership skills and the knack he had for getting people to work together. Eisenhower's actual hands-on experience was limited — he missed going overseas in World War I and only attained command of an infantry battalion in 1940. But he had an uncanny ability to look at the big picture, and his organizational skills were superb. (General Douglas MacArthur called him the best staff officer in the army.) A brigadier general when the war began, Eisenhower was soon called to Washington by General George C. Marshall to lead the American army's War Plans Division. Promotion was swift after that — to major general in March 1942 and then to lieutenant general and officer commanding American forces in Europe in June 1942. As the top

man at the Supreme Headquarters, Allied Expeditionary Force, Eisenhower was particularly skilled at reconciling opposing points of view during the planning for Normandy — and balancing the sometimes fractious relationships between the British and American soldiers, airmen and sailors under his command.

Bernard Law Montgomery (above, right) had a reputation as a first-rate trainer of troops. In August 1942, Winston Churchill appointed him commander of the 8th Army. Morale among the troops there was low, and his opponent was the seemingly unbeatable General Erwin Rommel. By marshaling his forces and combining drive with caution, Montgomery defeated the Germans at the battle of El Alamein in November 1942. It was both a strategic victory, and a psychological one. As Winston Churchill put it: "Before Alamein, we never had a victory. After Alamein, we never had a defeat." Montgomery led the 8th Army on to Sicily and the invasion of Italy. But already critics were beginning to question the sometimes too-slow pace of his actions. Under Eisenhower, Montgomery commanded all ground forces in the initial stages of the D-Day invasion.

American General George C. Marshall and British General Sir Alan Brooke — were among the initial serious contenders. Air Chief Marshal Sir Arthur Tedder was made deputy SAC. All three service commanders in chief were British too. Montgomery would lead the Allied armies. Admiral Ramsay, organizer of the North African and Sicilian invasions, would command the vast Allied armada that was to bombard the French coast and deliver the troops in Operation Neptune. Air Chief Marshal Sir Trafford Leigh-Mallory would lead the Allied tactical air forces. General Omar Bradley would command American troops under Montgomery.

Both Eisenhower and Montgomery regarded a three-division front as inadequate. The planners would have preferred four, with Caen and the high ground between the city and Falaise (needed for fighter airfields) as primary objectives, followed by a swing west to take Cherbourg. Ike and Monty, apparently simultaneously, decided to land five divisions across a fifty-mile front. The expansion entailed a postponement to early June, as well as deferment of what was intended to be the preliminary invasion of the south of France (Operation Dragoon). There were insufficient landing craft for both operations together — not to mention for the U.S. invasion of the Marianas Islands in the Pacific planned for June 15, with an assault wave only 22,500 men smaller than Overlord's.

In January 1944, Montgomery set up his headquarters at St. Paul's School in Hammersmith, west London (of which he happened to be a former pupil), took a small flat nearby and surrounded himself with staff from his successful North African campaign. The COSSAC organization was disbanded, though most members remained with Montgomery or with Eisenhower (who likewise chose key staff he knew from earlier operations).

The essence of Montgomery's plan was for one Canadian and two British divisions to attack three beaches near Caen in the east — tackling the main German strength, in particular the armored forces — while two American divisions, one strongly reinforced, assaulted two beaches to the west. One British and two American airborne divisions would secure the flanks to east and west respectively. The Americans would use their armor to break out from the bridgehead, take Cherbourg and swing south to the river Loire and then east toward the river Seine and Paris, while the British advanced more slowly eastward toward the Seine in the north. The ultimate objective of the Normandy campaign was to seize all the bridges over the Seine from the coast to Paris.

After their breakout, superior U.S. manpower would enable the Americans to pour in the bulk of Allied reinforcements. The east-west assignment of the landing beaches reflected the positions of the military camps along the south coast of England, with the Americans in the west and the Anglo-Canadians to the east. This arrangement also made it easier for the U.S. to supply its forces by sea direct from America. The boundary line between the 2nd British and 1st American armies (hence "21st" Army Group) in Normandy would run roughly due south from the city of Bayeux.

With uncharacteristic boldness, Montgomery decided to go for all three initial objectives in phase one. Caen was to be captured on D-Day itself, and the plateau to the southeast immediately thereafter. The Americans were to cut off the Cotentin Peninsula and isolate, then capture, Cherbourg as soon as possible. Then a steadily expanding bridgehead would spread inexorably across the face of northwest France, as Montgomery's own campaign map clearly forecast. The target line for D-Day+14 embraced Caen and the high ground beyond. Unfortunately, the Germans, like most enemies, would write their own script, ensuring that events failed to conform to Allied plans in many fundamental respects — especially in the early days of the Normandy campaign.

But as Montgomery told BBC Radio years later in his retirement:
> My plan was to threaten to break out on the eastern flank…in the Caen sector. Now, by pursuing this threat relentlessly, I intended to draw the main enemy reserves and particularly his armored divisions into this sector and to keep them there, and this was to be the job of the 2nd British Army under General Dempsey.… Having got the main enemy strength committed…on the eastern flank, my plan was to make the breakout on the western flank, using the 1st American Army under General Bradley.… I reckoned we would be on the general line of the Seine within three months — that would be by D+90.

WHILE THE GRAND STRATEGY OF OVERLORD CAN BE PRESENTED RELA-tively simply, the devil was undoubtedly strongly represented in the details. The operational orders for Neptune (the assault phase and naval prelude to Operation Overlord) were the most elaborate of their kind ever written: nearly a thousand pages in a file three inches thick. They covered the deployment and movements of 1,212 warships, 4,026 landing ships and craft of all sizes, 731 ancillary vessels and 864 merchant ships taken up from trade — the largest invasion fleet ever assembled. The British and Canadian navies supplied seventy-eight percent of the warships, the Americans seventeen percent and other Allied navies the rest.

The plans were put together by British Rear Admiral George Creasy, chief of staff to Admiral Ramsay, who oversaw every detail. Nobody had a greater personal and emotional stake in the invasion than Ramsay — a brisk, slightly built Lowland Scot. And nobody made a greater contribution to its success.

Now sixty-one, Ramsay had organized the successful evacuation of a third of a million British and Allied troops from Dunkirk in Operation Dynamo, for which he was knighted. Four years and two days after it ended, he would take the British army back to northwest France with its allies. Designated Vice Admiral, Dover, in 1938 in the event of war, Ramsay had been on the retired list since apparently ruining his career by resigning in 1935 as chief of staff to the commander in chief, Home Fleet, because his advice had been ignored. (Irrepressible certitude was one of several qualities he shared with Montgomery.)

He was officially still on the retired list when assigned to Overlord. In fact, it was only on Churchill's intervention with King George VI and the Admiralty that Ramsay was restored to the navy's active list in time for Neptune, ending an absurd, bureaucratic anomaly. By then he was Britain's acknowledged master of amphibious warfare, outclassing Admiral Mountbatten, the British chief of Combined Operations responsible for Dieppe, who was reassigned to Southeast Asia in October 1943.

As naval commander in chief, Ramsay not only was responsible for the seaborne assault phase of Overlord but also formed a mutual admiration society with Montgomery after initial clashes and became the main driving force behind the entire preparatory process — and this, in the teeth of disagreements among and

between Allied commanders and politicians. One of those rare individuals who could see the forest and the trees at the same time, Ramsay was famous for the clarity of his briefings, whether of politicians, generals or journalists. Questions were seldom, if ever, necessary.

His apparently insatiable demands for more air support and ships, especially landing craft, drew the disapproval of his contemporaries from other services, who were no less demanding. The landing-craft dispute was chronic, especially since so many were needed simultaneously in the Pacific. While the Americans criticized Ramsay for underloading them, their experience was in the warmer and usually more benign Pacific. The British admiral had the treacherous Channel to contend with. D-Day had been postponed from the end of April 1944 so that another month's prodigious landing-craft production could be added to the invasion fleet. Even so, the plan to mount a subsidiary invasion of the south of France on or before D-Day had to be dropped, largely for lack of sufficient landing craft. It could only be launched ten weeks later.

The Germans anticipated the Allies' desperate need for at least one major port through which they could pass the huge mass of reinforcements, supplies and equipment required to establish and maintain their armies on the Continent. The main ports of occupied Western Europe were therefore strongly defended. The Dieppe disaster proved that seizing such a port was likely to be far too costly in casualties, something that had been worrying Churchill since 1942.

The solution was a remarkable piece of lateral thinking — artificial harbors, code-named "Phoenix" but better known as "Mulberries." Two were prepared, consisting of a total of 213 concrete caissons measuring up to two hundred feet by fifty-five feet and weighing six thousand tons. Army engineers supervised the construction, while the navy took care of planning, delivery and assembly. Some twenty thousand workers in ports around southern England completed the work in seven months. The "harbors" were to be towed across to the Normandy coast and sunk in place, with sixty scuttled blockships ("Gooseberries") to act as breakwaters during installation and to fill gaps. The anticipated, if much underestimated, need for fuel for thousands of vehicles and aircraft was partly dealt with by PLUTO (Pipe Line Under The Ocean). This supply line, laid by ships bearing huge reels of pipe, would bring

(Above) A watercolor by American war artist Dwight Shepler chronicles the construction of a "Mulberry" artificial harbor at the Portsmouth Shipyard in April 1944. After the invasion, these enormous concrete structures, weighing several thousand tons, would be towed across the Channel at three to four knots and then sunk to form the breakwaters and piers needed by the attack forces.

in huge quantities of fuel every day, sharply reducing the need for vulnerable and cumbersome tankers.

Symptomatic of the omnivorous attention to detail called for by the greatest of invasions was the appeal to the British public for holiday photographs taken on Continental beaches before the war. No fewer than ten million snapshots were sent in. High-level and low-level photographic reconnaissance continued throughout the months preceding the invasion, seldom troubled by a much diminished Luftwaffe that had been swallowed up on other fronts. By D-Day, Allied air superiority was overwhelming — as essential a prerequisite for success as Britain's naval supremacy in the Channel.

THE ANGLO-AMERICAN ALLIANCE, INEVITABLY PERHAPS, WAS BEDEVILED BY DIFFERENCES OF outlook and personality clashes at all levels — both between and within the governments and armed forces of each ally. Nowhere was this more pronounced than in the air. Tension among the air commanders, between them and Montgomery as ground c-in-c, and between the British and Americans rose as the planning and the campaign itself ran into difficulties. Through Air Chief Marshal Leigh-Mallory, his air c-in-c, Eisenhower had control of the RAF's 2nd and the USAAF's 9th tactical air forces, which flew fighters and light and medium bombers in support of ground operations.

But the USAAF now outnumbered the RAF by two to one, and none of its senior commanders seemed ready to defer to Tedder, Eisenhower's deputy from the RAF — much less to Leigh-Mallory, a fighter man and no diplomat. Air Chief Marshal Sir Arthur Harris of RAF Bomber Command and Lieutenant General Carl Spaatz of the U.S. Army's 8th Air Force — whose joint task was to bomb Germany (by night and by day respectively) — were not under Eisenhower's command. As each believed Germany could be defeated by bombing alone, they had to be "persuaded" to divert their heavy bombers to support Overlord. Air Marshal Sir Arthur Coningham, commanding the 2nd Tactical Air Force, RAF, hated Spaatz and (especially) Montgomery. Lieutenant General Lewis Brereton, commanding the 9th Tactical Air Force, USAAF, loathed Coningham and refused to be junior to him in the Byzantine leadership structure of the Allied air forces.

Although Eisenhower was able to go over Spaatz's head to win over General Henry "Hap" Arnold, chief of staff of the USAAF, he could not get anywhere with Harris, or even Churchill, on this issue — until he dramatically threatened to resign in March 1944. He insisted on temporary command of the strategic bombers for the "Transportation Plan," drawn up to destroy the infrastructure of northern France in advance support of Overlord. The British were anxious about the potentially catastrophic cost in French civilian casualties. Only when both President Roosevelt and General de Gaulle, the Free French leader, accepted a high level of such "collateral damage" as unavoidable did Churchill agree. After that, Harris proved surprisingly amenable, more so than Spaatz. In all, nearly eight thousand Allied aircraft would be operational on D-Day.

THE PLANNING OF OVERLORD CHANGED MILLIONS OF LIVES, AS WHOLE ARMIES, FLEETS AND AIR forces were redeployed and went into intensive training. Generals were not immune. The fact that Major General Sir Percy Hobart was Montgomery's brother-in-law and raised the 7th Armoured Division (the famous "Desert Rats") had not saved him from forced early retirement. "Hobo" Hobart was one of the few Britons who understood armored warfare, but his unorthodoxy had annoyed some superiors. Exiled from command, he rose to the rank of lance corporal in the Home Guard, Britain's anti-invasion volunteers, until personally recalled by Churchill. COSSAC asked him to organize close armored support for the infantry at the very moment they were at their most vulnerable — coming up the beach.

No one envied Air Chief Marshal Trafford Leigh-Mallory (top) the contentious job of planning — and controlling — the air cover required for Operation Overlord. (Above) Major General Sir Percy "Hobo" Hobart developed a series of innovative tanks for use on the beaches of Normandy and sent them into battle as commander of the specially created 79th Armoured Division.

His answer was the DD (duplex-drive) tank, nicknamed "Donald Duck" by the troops — powered by propellers in water, where it was kept afloat by an inflatable buoyancy collar, but driven by its tracks on land. He quickly formed and trained the 79th Armoured Division in 1943, equipping it not only with DDs but also with outlandish tanks that carried portable bridges, rolls of matting for "roadways" across sand or mud, flails against mines or other specialized attachments. The unorthodox vehicles were collectively known as "Hobart's Funnies" and proved of enormous value to the British and Canadian assault troops. The Americans deployed only DD tanks on their beaches but later created their own funny tank, the "Rhinoceros" — a standard Sherman tank equipped with steel "horns" to uproot Normandy's stubborn hedgerows.

Hobart's Funnies

Each of Hobart's specialized armored vehicles was designed to perform a specific task during the invasion. (Right) One AVRE (Armoured Vehicle Royal Engineers) featured a "petard," an enormous howitzer. Used at close range, it could lob a high-explosive charge at a concrete seawall or the side of a bunker. (Below, left) The most common of all the Funnies, the DD (duplex-drive) tank was equipped with propellers and waterproof canvas sides. It could propel itself through the water as it accompanied the first waves of infantry, then drive onto the beach, drop its sides and fight as a normal tank. (Middle, top) The flail tank boasted a revolving drum equipped with chains to blow up mines. (Middle, bottom) This innovative advance vehicle laid a roadway on the landing beaches for the tanks following behind. (Below, right) The massive charges fired by the petard.

CHAPTER TWO

A Grand Deception

"In order to deceive and baffle the enemy as well as to exercise our forces, there will be many false alarms, many feints and many dress rehearsals."

— Winston Churchill, from an address to the nation, March 26, 1944

■ THE BRIEFEST GLANCE AT THE MAP of the Channel area shows that the Pas de Calais, the part of northwest France around the port of that name, is closest to England — only twenty-one miles by sea from Dover. This was therefore the most heavily fortified and most densely manned coastal zone in the Europe of 1944. The Wehrmacht knew an invasion was inevitable in view of the success of Operation Torch and the continuing American buildup in Britain. And the Allies could hardly prevent the Germans from drawing the obvious conclusion. Therefore, the main task of Allied (principally British) intelligence agencies from spring 1943 was to keep them guessing — not only about when but, even more importantly, about where.

Adolf Hitler prided himself on his intuition. In 1943 he was convinced that Normandy, although some one hundred miles south of England across a treacherous seaway, would be the invasion target. His commander in chief in the west, the venerable and experienced Field Marshal Gerd von Rundstedt, shared this opinion. Both, however, came around to the view that there would be a diversionary assault on Normandy to mask the real one against the Pas de Calais. As a result, this area remained more heavily defended than Normandy, to its southwest. It was also the strongest section of the much-vaunted "Atlantic Wall," which ran the length of the Dutch, Belgian and French coasts facing Britain. In fact, this was no wall but, rather, a series of concrete defensive structures — including casemates for coastal guns with underground shelters for their crews, blockhouses and pillboxes on and overlooking beaches, observation bunkers and strongpoints either specially built or else concealed behind or even inside seaside buildings. By 1942, some 250,000 men were working on these immovable fortifications — many of which can still be seen — and pouring eight hundred thousand tons of concrete per month into them.

(Above) A German soldier stands guard at one of the thousands of concrete bunkers that were erected along the length of the Atlantic Wall. (Opposite) The battery at Longues-sur-Mer has been preserved with its guns intact.

Hitler and von Rundstedt were encouraged to persist in their miscalculation — not only before and during the invasion, but also well after it — by the most sustained campaign of deception in military history. A campaign that would prove to be a major factor in the outcome of the Normandy invasion, and of the war as a whole.

IN NOVEMBER 1943, FIELD MARSHAL ROMMEL WAS GIVEN DIRECT RESPONSIBILITY FOR repelling an invasion. He was also given command of Army Group B, whose area included the continental coastal regions closest to Britain. Unlike Hitler and von Rundstedt, Rommel kept a more open mind about the likely target of the invaders. His strategy was

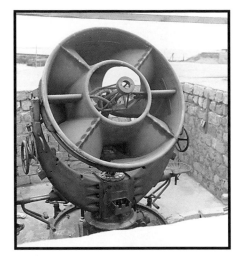

simple — to stop them on the beaches with specially designed obstacles wherever they struck, and to hit them hardest during the initial landing phase when they were most exposed. Von Rundstedt wanted to keep the crucial panzer (armored) divisions in reserve for a massive counterattack. Rommel — who believed Allied air superiority would hamper, if not cripple, such a delayed response — was undoubtedly encouraged in his strategy of forward defense by the near-disaster of the Allied landing at Anzio on the west coast of Italy in January 1944, when infantry without armor were mowed down.

Unfortunately for him, he was under specific orders not to commit the panzers without permission from von Rundstedt and/or Hitler himself. Such fatal differences among the German high command compounded the effect of the Allied deception scheme.

It was clear from Hitler's War Directive number 51 of November 3, 1943, that the Germans fully expected an invasion in 1944 — not least because they planned a second blitz on Britain with the new "Vengeance" V1 flying bombs to be launched from northern France. The thirty-seven German divisions in France and the Low Countries in October 1943 had risen to forty-eight in January 1944 and to fifty-six in June, with two extra panzer divisions earmarked for transfer from the eastern front if necessary. The increase from October 1943 was no more than a reversal of the Wehrmacht's previous policy of plundering its western garrisons to reinforce in the east. The overall number of German divisions rose to 328 in October 1943 — although the average strength of a division sank well below Anglo-American, if not Russian, levels. Some were forty percent below even German norms.

(Left) Field Marshal Erwin Rommel, center, looks out to sea from one of the smaller gun emplacements along the French coast. (Top) A listening device at Cherbourg is angled skyward, ready to pick up the sounds of approaching Allied aircraft. (Above) Officers supervise artillery training in one of the coastal bunkers.

The German Generals — Rommel and von Rundstedt

Hitler put the defense of the western flank of his empire in the hands of two of his most competent generals. Although neither was a Nazi, both could be counted on to follow their leader's orders to the utmost.

The independent-minded Gerd von Rundstedt, at right, had in fact been forced out of the Wehrmacht in 1938. He was recalled by Hitler at the start of the war and commanded Army Group South during the invasion of Poland, then led forty-five divisions during the invasion of France. Von Rundstedt later served in Russia, where he resigned when Hitler forbade a tactical withdrawal late in 1941. He was reinstated in 1943 and sent to France as c-in-c, west, to oversee preparations against an Allied invasion — including the reinforcement of the Atlantic Wall.

Probably no German general is as well-known as Erwin Rommel, at left. A career officer (like von Rundstedt), Rommel served in the First World War and stayed on in the much shrunken German army of the 1920s. A theoretician and scholar, he had written a book on infantry tactics (which had impressed Hitler) — but it was in armored warfare that he made his mark. In 1940, Rommel was the commander of the 7th Panzer Division during the invasion of France. His troops moved faster and farther than any other army in history, swinging south toward the Spanish border after reaching the Channel. Promoted to general, he earned the nickname "Desert Fox" for his brilliant exploits in North Africa. Only at El Alamein in November 1942 did the tide turn against him. Two years later, in January 1944, Rommel was sent to France to spearhead the German army's defenses against a suspected Allied invasion.

AN OVERALL PLAN TO MISLEAD THE GERMANS ABOUT THE INTENTIONS OF THE WESTERN ALLIES — Operation Bodyguard — was agreed to at the Anglo-American summit in Cairo in December 1943. Within Bodyguard were several specifically targeted deception schemes. The scope, objectives and timing of Operation Overlord were masked by Operation Fortitude, which came in two parts: North and South. Fortitude North's job was to create the impression that the Allies planned to invade Norway in collaboration with the Russians (who cooperated enthusiastically). Scottish Command under Lieutenant General Sir Andrew Thorne and a few dozen energetic staff officers created a phantom "4th Army" of eight divisions, generating much spurious radio traffic for German eavesdroppers to monitor. Two divisions were supposed to invade the northerly port of Narvik while the rest concentrated on Stavanger in the south with a view to advancing on Oslo, the capital. Russian officers were seen in Edinburgh, their presence faithfully reported by German spies in Britain who had been detected and "turned," becoming double agents.

Two Norwegians sent to Scotland in 1943 to spy for the Germans defected on landing and were recruited to help foster the Fortitude North myth: they were christened Mutt and Jeff by their British handlers. Major units committed to Overlord did much of their training in Scotland, sustaining the pretense of a massive buildup in the north of Britain. This masquerade dovetailed neatly into Hitler's obsession with defending Norway, where he had concentrated considerable naval and military forces.

Fortitude South was a much grander deception. Once the place and provisional date of the invasion were chosen, the deceivers set out to delude the Germans into believing that the target area was the Pas de Calais — both to mask the timing and the true objective of the landing, and to persuade the enemy to keep his main forces focused on the Pas de Calais for at least two weeks after D-Day. When COSSAC gave way to SHAEF (Supreme Headquarters, Allied Expeditionary Force) on Eisenhower's arrival in London in January 1944, coordination of the deception effort was assigned to a London Controlling Section. The LCS liaised with the bewildering plethora of British and American intelligence agencies gathering information about the enemy from aerial reconnaissance, captured documents, prisoners, radio intercepts, codebreaking and espionage by agents and Resistance groups.

The starting point for both Fortitudes was to convince the Germans that there were more military forces in Britain than those actually present. A fictional First U.S. Army Group (FUSAG) of eleven divisions in four corps (150,000 troops), focused on the Pas de Calais and commanded by General Patton from an imaginary headquarters in Chelmsford, Essex, was created in southeast England. It boasted fake tanks and dummy landing craft, empty tents, artificial radio traffic and spoof airfields for the benefit of the handful of high-flying German reconnaissance fighters who dared to come over. There was also an entire dummy oil-tank farm near Dover, its mock containers designed by the architect Sir Basil Spence and made as realistic as possible by the magical illusionist Jasper Maskelyne.

Faking It

One of the key aims of Operation Bodyguard was to deceive the enemy about where the invasion would take place. Numerous deceptions were created to give the impression that a buildup was occurring elsewhere in Britain than along the south coast. (Opposite, top right) These landing craft looked real, but they could be assembled in a few hours. Unfortunately, they were so light that in high winds they blew away. (Opposite, top left) A jeep has been disguised to look like a tank. (Insets, opposite) The cloth "tank" (top) fitted onto a metal framework. (Middle) A soldier stands beside an inflatable version of a three-ton truck. (Bottom) Although jeeps were made to look like tanks, sometimes the opposite was needed. This boxy-looking truck is a tank in disguise. (Below) Shoulder patches designed for the American 18th and 135th Airborne Divisions — two of the units in the "phantom" First U.S. Army Group.

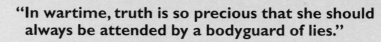

"In wartime, truth is so precious that she should always be attended by a bodyguard of lies."

— Winston Churchill

Master of Deception

Creating a dummy oil-tank farm was only one of many brilliant tricks up the sleeve of Jasper Maskelyne (below, in coffin) during the "deceptions" that preceded the Normandy invasion. Maskelyne — a third-generation stage magician, inventor and one of Britain's most popular illusionists — had been eager to serve his country when war broke out. He convinced a skeptical War Office of his usefulness by employing mirrors and a scale model to create the illusion that a

German battleship was sailing up the Thames. His first assignment was in North Africa, where he and a small group of hand-picked assistants created a series of ruses that helped confound the enemy. They built a replica of the city of Alexandria to divert German bombers; hid the Suez Canal with a system of dazzling spotlights; and created a dummy army to confuse Rommel about the true location of the British forces. Maskelyne's famous "magic gang" disbanded after the battle of El Alamein, but Maskelyne carried on his work with Operation Fortitude and other missions.

King George VI solemnly made a publicized tour of inspection. All this had to take place in the southeast of England because it was the only part of Britain that the weakened Luftwaffe could reconnoiter by fast fighter frequently and in relative safety. The deceivers even persuaded Patton to wine and dine a German prisoner-of-war general, being repatriated on health grounds, at his headquarters, where there was much unsubtle talk about the Pas de Calais.

A crucial role in selling the deception to the German intelligence services was played by an anti-Fascist, pro-British double agent from Spain code-named "Garbo." Juan Pujol Garcia, originally active in neutral Lisbon, was brought to London in spring 1942. He was allowed to include enough real information in his messages to convince the Abwehr (German military intelligence) and the German army's FHW (Foreign Armies West) bureau of his reliability. Garbo was ultimately allowed to send a D-Day invasion warning a few hours before the event — and another at the very moment when it began. Perhaps his greatest accolade was Hitler's personal decision in August 1944 to award him the Iron Cross *in absentia!*

At the same time, the Allies needed to conceal the movement of key units, such as the "Desert Rats" (the British 7th Armoured Division), from the Mediterranean to England. And the thrust of disinformation also had to be reversed. The false hints of an imminent invasion of France in 1943 (which worked well enough to achieve surprise for the invasion of Sicily) gave way in 1944 to the false rumor that there would not be one — at least not until late in the year.

MISLEADING THE GERMANS ABOUT THE INVASION AREA LED THE ALLIED air forces — the Americans by day and the British by night — to bomb key installations in the Pas de Calais area at least as heavily as those in Normandy as D-Day approached. An important target of the deception plan was the chain of forty-seven enemy radar stations along the coasts of northwest France. Professor R.V. Jones of RAF Intelligence, one of many "backroom boffins" involved in the war effort, thought the plan to deceive German radar was too simple and limited. In mid-April 1944, he complained to Eisenhower's deputy, Air Chief Marshal Tedder:

I told him what the problem was, that I had seen the plans for the invasion and they included attacks on radar stations but they weren't on a scale that was likely to be effective. The plan for the spoofing, which involved leaving one or two stations intact — I thought the scale was altogether too small. Tedder seemed reasonably convinced.

Tedder subsequently issued instructions to the air staff to expand the deception plan. Fighters were used to attack all the stations, but half a dozen were let off lightly — to be overwhelmed during the invasion by such ruses as "window" (aluminum-foil strips dropped by air that confused radar) or trawlers towing radar reflectors.

ABOUT A WEEK BEFORE D-DAY, IMMEDIATELY AFTER THE 7 P.M. AND 9 P.M. nightly news broadcasts, the BBC French Service began to broadcast, in deadpan tones, a series of outlandish messages. On the night of June 5–6, the exercise was repeated: an announcer droned through another collection of disjointed French messages, bemusing German eavesdroppers. The most famous, immortalized in the film *The Longest Day*, was a (misquoted) couplet by the poet Verlaine:

Les sanglots longs des violons de l'automne
Blessent mon coeur d'une langueur monotone.
[The heavy sobs of autumnal violins
Soothe my heart with a dull languor.]

The first line indicated that the invasion was about a week ahead; the second, that it would begin that night. Contrary to legend, these messages — prepared by the British Special Operations Executive, which ran agents in occupied territory — were not a call for a general uprising by the Resistance. Each message was aimed at a specific group; the second half confirmed that it should now execute a predetermined act of sabotage to distract and impede the Germans as the invasion began.

German counterintelligence had "turned" enough Allied and Resistance agents itself to know that these messages were invasion alerts. Its wireless interception station in Paris therefore alerted the 15th Army in the Pas de Calais and the 7th in Normandy. The former passed on the warning to subordinate units; the latter, doubtless tired of the many false alarms of recent months, did not.

"It is true that the hour of invasion draws nearer, but the scale of enemy air attacks does not indicate that it is immediately imminent."

— Field Marshal Gerd von Rundstedt, reporting to Hitler on May 30, 1944

Southampton's Berth 38 is one of the last of the city's piers that remains as it was in 1944. (Inset, opposite) Camouflaged landing craft fill Southampton's harbor in June 1944.

CHAPTER THREE

The Forerunners

**"The American presence had swollen that spring to almost all-pervading proportions,
so that there seemed more Americans than natives in the district."**

— Military historian John Keegan (then a ten-year-old schoolboy in England)

■ AS THE SPRING OF 1944 came and went in the United Kingdom, the country began more and more to resemble an armed camp. Hundreds of thousands of American and Canadian troops had arrived by sea to join the invasion forces. The British army was also building up its strength. So were the Allied air forces on airfields all over England, and the navies in ports on the western, eastern and southern coasts of the island of Great Britain. Hundreds of plywood gliders were assembled and lined up on the grass of bomber bases, ready to carry airborne troops and their equipment into battle. And many hundreds of temporary camps were set up behind barbed wire — not only all over the south of England but also as far away as the Highlands of Scotland, the moors of Wales, and northern and western England. These wilder areas were used for training, while the camps along or close behind the straggling coastline of southern England accommodated the military units bound for France.

The purpose of this unprecedented activity was obvious — but largely left unsaid. More and more British and foreign troops turned up at local dances or pubs on weekend passes, but the "careless talk" that notices everywhere warned "costs lives" was notable for its absence. Security was high, and in the last days of May verged on stifling as the troops were locked away altogether. Along England's south coast, the Allied forces carried out amphibious exercises of ever-increasing size and complexity. (One such night operation, at Slapton Sands, Devon, on April 28, 1944, went disastrously wrong. Fast German naval vessels attacked the landing craft, killing more than seven hundred American soldiers and sailors. To protect Operation Overlord, the casualties were buried in secret.)

Group Captain Stagg, Eisenhower's weatherman, moved from London to take up residence with the most senior commanders at Southwick House on May 28. As he and his American deputy, Colonel D. N. Yates, were driven southwest toward Portsmouth after many weeks of virtual confinement in their offices, they were profoundly impressed by the long lines of tanks, guns, trucks and jeeps on every highway and byway. Stagg wrote:

These endless miles of tanks and guns marshaled along the gentle summer lanes of Hampshire finally brought home to us the magnitude of our responsibility....

As the invasion date approached, the training of troops intensified throughout all of the Allied armies. (Above) These snapshots, belonging to former British paratrooper Eric "Bill" Sykes, show practice jumping in the spring of 1944. (Opposite) Canadian navy commandos during exercises in Scotland in the winter of 1943–44. (Inset) American troops come ashore at Slapton Sands.

"[We were] on a schedule of specialized training, which included chemical warfare, sniper techniques, tank operating, mines and booby traps, dispatch riding and antiaircraft defense."

— W. K. "Bill" Newell, W Commando, Royal Canadian Navy

(Left) Dwight Shepler documented one of the many practice attacks launched at Slapton Sands by the American forces in the months before the invasion. (Below) Marvin Perrett, a landing-craft coxswain aboard the USS Bayfield, witnessed the assault by German torpedo boats on an American convoy at Slapton Sands on April 28, 1944.

Tragedy — and Secrecy — at Slapton Sands

With its shallow lagoon backed by bluffs, Slapton Sands on Devon's south coast was the site of frequent invasion rehearsals by the U.S. Army because it most closely resembled Utah Beach on the Normandy coast. On April 27, 1944, some three hundred ships and thirty thousand American troops gathered at sea there for an exercise intended to be as realistic as possible — complete with a close-support barrage and tanks. Code-named Operation Tiger, it was the sixth in a planned series of seven rehearsals, each bigger than the last.

An American convoy of large LSTs (landing ship, tanks) entered and circled Lyme Bay after midnight on April 28, their only escort a single British corvette. (An additional destroyer, detailed to accompany them, had been damaged in a collision the day before and stayed in harbor.) Around 2 A.M., the convoy was attacked by nine fast German torpedo boats on a hit-and-run raid out of Cherbourg. Torpedoes slammed into three of the LSTs, setting off ammunition and fuel. Many soldiers, trapped below decks, perished. Those who jumped clear fared no better. None of the troops had been instructed on the correct way to wear their inflatable life belts. As a result, when the heavily laden soldiers hit the water with the belts around their waists, they flipped upside down and drowned.

Two of the LSTs sank and the third was badly damaged. Casualties included 198 seamen and 552 soldiers dead or missing, and 89 men wounded. Ironically, these numbers exceeded those suffered by the Americans during the actual assault on Utah Beach a few weeks later. To prevent the Germans from possibly learning about the impending invasion, the bodies of those lost at Slapton Sands were quickly buried — and nothing was revealed about the disaster until after the war.

CRAFTSMAN ARTHUR WILDMAN OF THE ROYAL ELECTRICAL AND MECHANICAL ENGINEERS managed to fit his wedding and a short honeymoon into the last leave period before the troops assigned to Overlord were locked into their camps for ten days for security reasons. Then life became tedious:

We were moved off, under canvas, to somewhere in Hampshire. That was very depressing because we were behind a barbed-wire fence and we were all in bell tents. And there were just rumors. We sealed the tanks and the vehicles some time before, against water. That was the first inkling I had, a fairly rushed job.... We used to hand our washing through the wire fence and get it done that way.... The worst part of any action is waiting. We all wanted to get on with it — sitting about with very little news coming through, it was really like being in limbo.

The feeling of frustration that descended on fit young men with very little to do except wait was occasionally relieved:

I remember Monty [visiting and he] spoke from a jeep, and he wouldn't allow people to come behind him. There were Redcaps [military police] right the way behind him in a semicircle.... I think there was a general air of cynicism about what came down from anyone of a high rank, and he made a remark that he never put troops into action unless he could win and win easily. And the way the press reported it, the suggestion was that there were never any casualties involved, and we laughed heartily to ourselves.

Trooper Roland Johnston was a gunner-driver in the 94th Battery, 3rd Antitank Regiment, Royal Canadian Artillery, bound for Juno Beach. His troop was equipped with two-pounder antitank guns:

We knew that we were going to go into battle. We were eager to go into battle. We were all eager. We were tired of training by the time the invasion came. We were glad to see it come, although I believe I can speak for most of the fellows [when I say] we were scared to hell.

THE ALLIED COMMAND FULLY UNDERSTOOD THE NEED TO KEEP THE "HOME FRONT" INFORMED OF the progress of the intended liberation of Europe. Elaborate arrangements were made to ensure massive, though always censored, coverage by press, radio and cinema newsreels. Commanders such as Eisenhower, Montgomery and Patton were always ready to provide what would now be called "sound bites" and "photo opportunities." They also gave quite detailed background briefings on their plans.

(Top) Cigarette in hand, Mike Ingrisano of the U.S. 316th Troop Carrier Group faces the camera as he and his buddies wait out the days before the invasion at their airfield in Cottesmore, England. (Above) Woodbines, the cheapest of all British cigarettes, were very popular with the Allied forces.

"**When the Regiment arrived here we found this camp was guarded and not by Canadian troops. All new vehicles and equipment were issued. All vehicles had to be waterproof and secrecy was the watchword. The mail all censored. One letter read like this: 'Dear Mum, cut-cut-cut, Love John.' No leaves were granted and we were told to make out our wills. Father Hickey came to say Mass, along with three other chaplains, and to hear confessions. Like the soldiers we were, we knew the signs. June I we arrived in Southampton.**"

— Rifleman J. P. Moore,
Queen's Own Rifles of Canada

(Above and left) Members of two sections of the mortar platoon from the Queen's Own Rifles of Canada, in a D-Day staging camp deep in England's New Forest.

The major American radio networks, newspapers, the BBC and news agencies committed large resources. Doon Campbell, future editor in chief of Reuters, was one of the agency's fifteen war correspondents assigned, "with one or two pigeons," to the invasion. In all there were about one hundred British and Canadian "assault correspondents"; the American media were also well represented. Montgomery personally briefed reporters on May 16: "He simply told us it would be a first-class party," Campbell remembered.

Since the reporters now knew more than almost anybody else about the invasion, he realized that "I would be sealed up, completely cut off from family, office, everybody. I was a non-person; I ceased to exist." He remembered almost falling off his chair when he opened the slip of paper with his assignment on it: "Campbell — Marine Commandos — D-Day." At the appointed time he reported to Brigadier Lord Lovat, of the 1st Special Service (Commando) Brigade that was to be one of the first units ashore:

> [Lovat] looked at me and my baggage and said, "You don't need that stuff." It was the stuff, actually, [with] which I had made do at [Monte] Cassino [the hardest Italian battle], but he said, "You'll get everything you need in a pack on your back." And I said, "Including a typewriter?" And he said, "Yes, including a typewriter."

THE INVASION WOULD ALSO BE THE SUPREME TEST FOR A POLITICALLY divided French Resistance. The Secret Army supporting General Charles de Gaulle and his government-in-exile in London; the ORA (Army Resistance Organization) committed to his rival, General Henri Giraud; and the Communist FTP (Francs-tireurs et partisans) were often at loggerheads. Giraud and de Gaulle's groups joined forces in spring 1943 in a National Council of Resistance, but the Communists kept their forces out of it while professing support for de Gaulle. This rivalry was a major headache for the British Special Operations Executive (SOE) that sent agents into occupied territory. The agents not only had to elude capture by the Germans — which could mean torture and death — but also needed to be diplomats as well as weapons, intelligence and wireless experts. But the imminent invasion at last produced the level of cooperation among Resistance groups needed for effective missions. By way of practice, the Resistance

(Above) During the Allies' first war conference in Casablanca in January 1943, rival French generals Henri Giraud, standing at left, and Charles de Gaulle, right, met under the watchful eye of Franklin D. Roosevelt and Winston Churchill.

paralyzed the infrastructure of Brittany, southwest of Normandy, including German communications, in May 1943, in support of Eisenhower's Transportation Plan.

SECURITY WAS NOT TOTAL IN FORTRESS BRITAIN. JOHN PHILLIPS WAS A SAILOR ABOARD A BRITISH minesweeper with a crew of two officers and twenty-three men. On a night out in Birkenhead at the beginning of June 1944, he was taken aback to be told — by no less an authority than some girls who worked in a local aircraft factory — that he was going to Plymouth the next day. Phillips was in an understandably skeptical mood when he encountered them in the same place the next evening, but the girls stuck to their prediction, adding that he would not be coming back to Merseyside. This time they were right. For a while, he did not expect to come back at all:

> *Our job was to sweep across, to widen the [Omaha] beachhead, put the lads ashore and that was our job finished, because I think we were a suicide squad…when we came back there was no mail…for us. There were other ships waiting by in Plymouth to take our place…. Looking back, I don't think we were supposed to come out.*

"We had a wonderful time actually because I think there were about thirteen thousand Americans up at the airport, which was just outside the town…. Probably seven thousand about five minutes' walk down the road in the other camp."

— Sadie Greaves, Women's Land Army

Sadie Greaves (left) was one of the thousands of young British women who helped work the land as members of the Women's Land Army (WLA) while the men were away at war. Although the government drive to enlist women made the WLA sound glamorous, the work was hard and many of the girls lived on isolated farms without electricity or running water. Chores included pest control (rat catching), potato planting and harvesting, apple picking and mending sacks. Sadie was stationed near Tavistock, Devon, and later just outside the lacemaking town of Honiton. "Everything was scarce and worth something in wartime," she remembers. Identity cards (right) had to be carried at all times, and all goods were rationed. Coupons for extras like a new dress were hard to come by. But Sadie found that Honiton was a good place for entertainment — especially with thousands of American soldiers stationed in camps nearby. "There were the ordinary dances and officers' dances in the local hall and we were asked to those. And really we did have a very good social life. So we had no complaints there at all."

Lieutenant Commander Ron Howard, RNR, was a man of many talents. Originally a trawler engineer, he was chosen by Admiral Ramsay himself for the key role of beach-master at one of the landing zones because of his stentorian voice. But he was also a trained frogman and canoeist. He had been on secret reconnaissance missions by submarine to beaches from Norway to Normandy. This is how he remembered one such trip, by X-craft (midget submarine):

> *When we were reconnoitering, they used to take us within three miles of low-water mark and we used to leave her submerged…and go ashore, reconnoitering up the beaches and taking the samples of sand in little canvas bags and fetching them back, and then being towed back by a trawler in the early hours of the morning. We only spent an hour on the beach.*

Late on June 4, he once again squeezed himself into midget sub *X-20*, which was to deliver him to Gold Beach and then take up station offshore (as did *X-23* nearby) to shine a light out to sea as a beacon for the incoming invasion fleet. The twenty-four-hour postponement to June 6 meant an uncomfortable extra night in the cramped boat, whose forty-foot length barely offered enough space for its normal crew of four.

(Above, left) General Eisenhower pays a surprise visit on June 5 to the men of the American 101st Airborne Division. (Top right) Members of the 82nd Airborne Division run a last check on their equipment before boarding their planes. (Above, right) American soldiers and sailors gather for an outdoor Roman Catholic mass at Weymouth, England. (Opposite, top) American rangers march along the seafront at Weymouth. (Bottom) Four officers from the 22nd Independent Parachute Company — the pathfinders for the 6th Airborne Division — synchronize their watches. Lieutenant Bobby de la Tour, far left, would earn the distinction of being the first British soldier in Normandy on June 6, 1944.

In advance of the main force, parachute units dropped "pathfinders" with lights and flares, portable radar and radio equipment so that they could spy out the drop zone and guide incoming aircraft. Rolland Duff of the 507th Regiment, 82nd Airborne Division, was a member of a team — or "stick"— of twenty-one men who arrived over Amfreville in a C-47 aircraft on the afternoon of June 5:

> *We were dropped exactly on target.… I dropped in an orchard which was a short distance from Amfreville and from a German garrison post.… The lieutenant who jumped ahead of me broke both of his feet and he was captured. The second in command, Lieutenant Ames, took over the group and seven of us assembled at the point where we were to set up our ground-to-air communications, our radar equipment.… We were being attacked by small-arms fire.*

The communications gear was set up at the right place by the right time, 7:30 P.M. on June 5.

British agent Red Wright was one of the earliest heralds of the invasion. On May 27, 1944, he was among a group of scouts who went ashore, four at a time in rubber dinghies, to link up with the French Resistance, who supplied them with old clothes and false papers. Such disguise meant they risked being summarily shot as spies if caught by the occupation authorities. Armed only with pocket pistols, Wright and his comrades casually walked several times over the two bridges that carried the narrow country road from Bénouville over the Caen Canal and across the river Orne to Ranville. As they walked, the men memorized the local landscape and defensive features. These bridges were one of the keys to the coming struggle.

To resemble agricultural laborers and to repel close inspection, Wright and his men had applied bran and farmyard muck to their borrowed clothes. On one of his walks, however, Wright was shot in the back without warning:

> *Most of the gendarmes knew and were friendly [about] what was going on.…*
> *We were just told that if we couldn't answer a particular question, to wave your*
> *hand in front of your face, turn your back and walk away. About two days*
> *before D-Day I did this after being approached by a gendarme, and as I walked*
> *away — bang! I felt a shot…in the shoulder.… Eventually I got an apology*
> *from the gendarme. I was never told the reason why the shot was fired.*

The French Resistance carried out nearly one thousand acts of sabotage on the night of June 5–6, a major contribution to the successful establishment of the Allied bridgehead.

IF ANY OF THIS ACTIVITY REGISTERED ON THE GERMAN COMMAND, THEY DIDN'T SHOW IT. FIELD Marshal Rommel went home on leave to Herrlingen near Ulm in Swabia, southwest Germany, on Sunday, June 4, to celebrate his wife Luise's birthday on the sixth and then to pay a brief call on Hitler. The weather in northern France was reassuringly bad, and he confidently left the temporary command of Army Group B — at La Roche-Guyon on the Seine, west of Paris — to his competent chief of staff, Lieutenant General Hans Speidel. Other key German commanders were also absent from their posts on Monday, June 5 — among them, Colonel General Friedrich Dollmann, commander of the 7th Army, whose area was about to be invaded, and SS General Sepp Dietrich of the I SS Panzer Corps. At least a dozen other senior commanders had gone for war games to Rennes in Brittany, southwest of Normandy.

AS THE LITTLE GROUPS OF FORERUNNERS CARRIED OUT THEIR PREPARATORY WORK FOR THE TROOPS approaching by sea, and the German commanders slept far from their Atlantic front, the men of three Allied airborne divisions took off from their bases in southern England to an intricate flight timetable. Among the first in the air were groups of troop-bearing gliders towed by bombers, all sporting the three broad white Allied aircraft-recognition stripes on wings and fuselage.

(Above and opposite) Members of the U.S. 2nd Ranger Battalion load onto landing craft in Weymouth, England, en route to Omaha Beach. Together with the British commandos, the American rangers had been given the difficult job of securing key points of the invasion beaches and silencing any German artillery batteries.

CHAPTER FOUR

Pegasus Bridge

■ THE FIRST ALLIED VICTORY on the soil of German-occupied France was achieved by 180 British airborne infantrymen and engineers delivered by half a dozen wooden gliders a few minutes after midnight on the night of June 5–6. They were the advance guard of the British 6th Airborne Division, formed barely fifteen months earlier and made up of one air-landing (glider-borne) and two paratroop brigades. The division's task was to seal the eastern flank of the invasion front. To do so, it had to seize three initial objectives. The "Red Berets" were ordered to capture intact the two bridges, seven hundred yards apart, across the Caen Canal and the roughly parallel river Orne, in order to be able to move forces around Caen; to destroy the bridges over the river Dives, five miles east of the drop zone, to hamper German counterattacks; and to seize the

battery of heavy coastal guns at Merville, removing a threat to Sword Beach from the east.

To deliver the division, the RAF needed 733 aircraft and 355 gliders. Six of the latter, piloted by sergeants of the Glider Pilot Regiment, were assigned to land Major John Howard's reinforced company from the 2nd Battalion, the Oxfordshire and Buckinghamshire Light Infantry, plus a platoon of Royal Engineers from 249 Field Company, as close as possible to the bridges that carried the road from Bénouville to Ranville over the canal and the Orne.

The countryside chosen for the landing — the estuary of the river Orne — was mostly flat and open with generally few trees (apart from the occasional small wood), marshy in some places,

A Horsa glider, sporting its distinctive white invasion stripes, is hauled slowly aloft by a British bomber.

"Not to worry, Major. I can slip between the poles quite easily, and by losing a wingtip off the port and a bit off the starboard, it could quite handily help slow us down."

— Glider pilot James Wallwork, discussing German antiglider obstacles with Major John Howard on June 3

deliberately flooded by the Germans in others. In many fields regarded as likely landing places for paratroops or gliders, the Germans had planted "Rommel's asparagus" — poles linked by wires and sometimes embellished with a mine. The pilots turned these obstacles partly to their own advantage by using them to slow down their craft on landing. The consequent damage increased the risk of injury to crew and complement but was otherwise irrelevant. Gliders were expendable — intended for a single, one-way trip into battle — and their pilots were to fight as infantry after landing.

The gliders were hauled painfully slowly into the air at Tarrant Rushton Airfield in Dorset by six Halifax bombers that began to take off at one-minute intervals from 2245 on June 5. Then they carefully circumvented the sprawling Allied armada

poised off the north Normandy coast for fear of friendly antiaircraft fire. The glider pilots released their gliders at six thousand feet and about three miles short of their target. The "tugs" then headed southwest to bomb Caen. At about the same time, around midnight, other aircraft dropped a total of sixty pathfinders in small groups across the 6th Airborne Division's designated deployment area, to seek out landing zones and guide the main drops with flares.

The lead glider, piloted by Sergeant James H. Wallwork, carried Major Howard and twenty-nine of his men, who sang soldiers' songs for most of the way across. As the thrum of the tug's engines faded quickly away, so did the singing. The tense rows of heavily laden troops braced themselves for the shock of landing by linking arms

"Right on Target, and Right on Time"

Staff Sergeant James H. Wallwork (top left) and his co-pilot, John Ainsworth, were both thrown through the perspex nose of the lead glider as they brought it hurtling in from six thousand feet. As Wallwork recalls:

"We removed a couple of fences and arrived as required at, or rather, in the embankment. Made an awful noise but seems afterwards not to have bothered the German sentries who thought perhaps part of a shot-down bomber had landed. Johnnie and I were stunned and pinned under the collapsed cockpit. But the troops had traveled fairly well and got on with it. Exactly one minute later, No. 2 arrived and joined in, followed by No. 3...."

Geoff Barkway (bottom left), at the controls of No. 3 glider with co-pilot Peter B. Boyle (middle left), hit the target as well — but "the force of the landing catapulted me through the front window and I landed in marshy water." Once on his feet, Barkway returned to the downed glider and helped extricate Boyle, who was unhurt but pinned down in the wreckage. The men later made their way to Pegasus Bridge, where Barkway was badly hit in the right arm by German fire. (He subsequently lost his arm.)

Thanks to the incredible skill and daring of the twelve glider pilots in the first assault wave, both bridges were captured quickly and held until the arrival of Lord Lovat's commandos some thirteen hours later. (Below, right) An aerial view of the landed gliders close by Pegasus Bridge.

"Long afterwards we all confessed to feeling rather pleased with ourselves at having pulled it off."

— James Wallwork, Glider Pilot Regiment

52

(Above) Major John Howard. In the film, *The Longest Day*, Howard was played by actor Richard Todd (below), a lieutenant with the 7th Battalion, the Parachute Regiment, during D-Day. (Right) Two of the three gliders that carried Howard's men lie on the ground not far from the canal bridge. In the background at right stands the Café Gondrée.

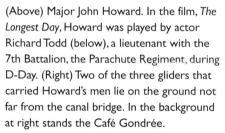

and raising their feet off the floor as the wooden frame and plywood body of the glider creaked and sighed through the unpowered descent. It seemed to take an age but it was only six minutes until the craft hit the ground at ninety miles per hour, crashing through ground obstacles and vegetation and scrunching across the wet earth until they slowed to a stop. Remarkably few suffered more than a shaking-up or bruising in the process. The only factor they had not met in training was the "asparagus," which was less threatening than it appeared. It was possible to slice through or knock down the poles without drastic consequences.

After the steep descent, Wallwork managed to come to a halt less than fifty yards from the bridge over the canal — an astonishing feat of navigation by the pilots of both tug and glider in moonlight obscured by partial cloud cover. (The Allied air c-in-c, Air Chief Marshal Leigh-Mallory, went so far as to describe it as the finest piece of flying in the entire war.) The second and third gliders hit the ground a little farther from the canal, again at one-minute intervals.

In all, four craft landed as planned but one came down half a mile away and the sixth crashed at least eight miles from its designated landing zone. (The men aboard marched and fought hard that night to rejoin their comrades.) Only one man died of injuries caused by the often-violent glider landings. With the ninety men immediately to hand, Major Howard stormed the canal bridge, killing or wounding German defenders too surprised to take concerted action. Armed only with light infantry weapons — submachine guns, rifles, hand- and smoke-grenades — his men dived into the trenches and sandbagged positions of the

Liberation at Last

Three-year-old Arlette Gondrée (right), her sister Georgette (left) and their parents, Georges and Thérèse (who aided British intelligence), hid in the cellar of their home, the Café Gondrée, near Pegasus Bridge on the night of June 5, 1944:

"Someone was walking above our heads. We thought the Germans were coming to get us. We were terrified. My father walked…from the cellar and opened the door. He was faced by two British soldiers who said, 'It is all right, chum. We have arrived. We are British soldiers.'… My mother started kissing them. They gave us some chocolate and biscuits and one of them picked me up. We all came upstairs and my father opened the front door of the café wide. Wounded were brought in on stretchers and our dining room became the operating theater.…"

German garrison, fighting hand to hand with the soldiers they had not shot or blasted. Other soldiers rushed the enemy guard posts on the bridge itself before moving on to subject the Orne bridge to similar treatment.

Lieutenant Den Brotheridge, however, was shot dead as he led a rush across the canal bridge — the first Briton to fall to enemy action in the Normandy campaign. It was this unusual crossing, with its prominent motorized hinge at one end for lifting the single span clear of shipping, that would be immortalized as "Pegasus Bridge" in honor of the airborne troops' winged-horse badge. (The Orne bridge was styled "Horsa," after the type of glider used by the attackers.)

Immediately after the initial success, Howard's force repeatedly transmitted the pre-arranged signal that both bridges had been taken intact: "Ham and jam. Ham and jam…" By then the engineers had searched the bridge but had not discovered any explosive charges. (They were later found stored in a nearby building.) Meanwhile the infantrymen took up defensive positions to await counterattacks — and the reinforcements that were scheduled to drop by parachute within half an hour. More gliders would bring supplies and munitions. The bridges are in open country; if the citizens of the nearby villages of Bénouville and Ranville heard what was going on as the British arrived, they did not show themselves.

Although the original Pegasus Bridge was replaced in 1994, the current structure (right) is remarkably similar to the bridge that was captured by Major Howard and his men (insets, left and right). To the far left of the bridge stands the Café Gondrée, which still welcomes visitors today. It was the first building in France to be liberated by the Allies.

"My father asked the British soldiers digging in the vegetable patch to unearth the precious wine and champagne he had buried during the occupation, to comfort the poor wounded...and to drink [all together] to celebrate our liberation."

— Arlette Gondrée, who still lives at the Café Gondrée

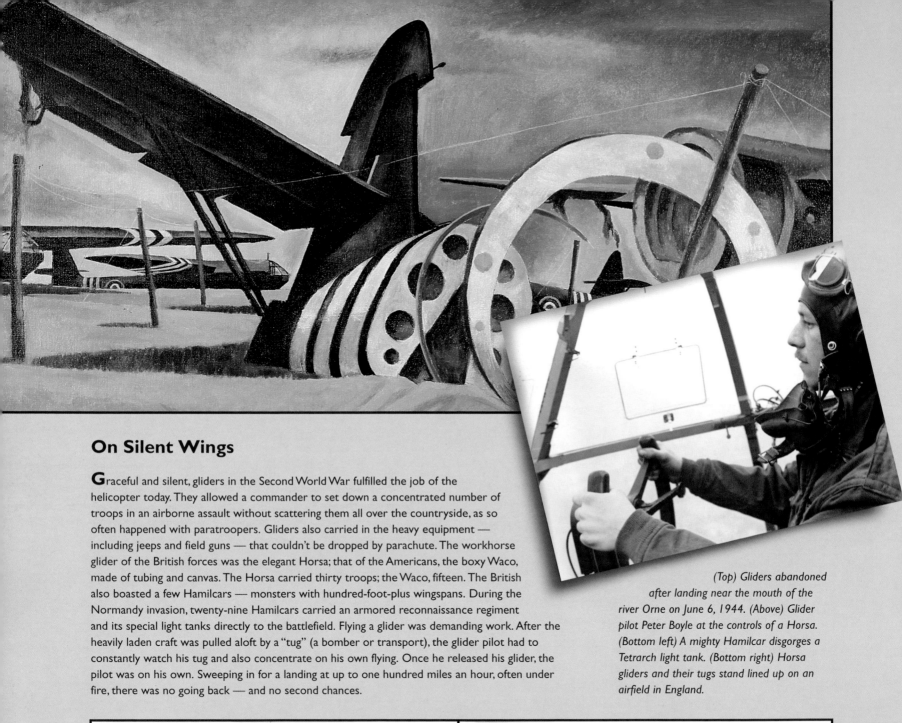

On Silent Wings

Graceful and silent, gliders in the Second World War fulfilled the job of the helicopter today. They allowed a commander to set down a concentrated number of troops in an airborne assault without scattering them all over the countryside, as so often happened with paratroopers. Gliders also carried in the heavy equipment — including jeeps and field guns — that couldn't be dropped by parachute. The workhorse glider of the British forces was the elegant Horsa; that of the Americans, the boxy Waco, made of tubing and canvas. The Horsa carried thirty troops; the Waco, fifteen. The British also boasted a few Hamilcars — monsters with hundred-foot-plus wingspans. During the Normandy invasion, twenty-nine Hamilcars carried an armored reconnaissance regiment and its special light tanks directly to the battlefield. Flying a glider was demanding work. After the heavily laden craft was pulled aloft by a "tug" (a bomber or transport), the glider pilot had to constantly watch his tug and also concentrate on his own flying. Once he released his glider, the pilot was on his own. Sweeping in for a landing at up to one hundred miles an hour, often under fire, there was no going back — and no second chances.

(Top) Gliders abandoned after landing near the mouth of the river Orne on June 6, 1944. (Above) Glider pilot Peter Boyle at the controls of a Horsa. (Bottom left) A mighty Hamilcar disgorges a Tetrarch light tank. (Bottom right) Horsa gliders and their tugs stand lined up on an airfield in England.

The cap badge of the Parachute Regiment.

The 5th Parachute Brigade (three battalions of the Parachute Regiment) under Brigadier Nigel Poett began to land on time to consolidate Howard's coup de main on the bridges, which had taken just under fifteen minutes. The airborne position at the vital crossings was to be relieved and further reinforced by seaborne troops — initially by Brigadier Lord Lovat's Commando Brigade, and finally by conventional infantry on the sixth.

The 7th Parachute Battalion began landing in sticks of twenty-one men each from adapted British Stirling bombers of 620 Squadron, RAF. But the drops were scattered over a wide area and at first only half the battalion — some three hundred men — was available to reinforce Howard. Among them was Lieutenant Richard Todd, the actor who would play Major Howard in Darryl F. Zanuck's 1962 D-Day epic, *The Longest Day*:

When we were getting very near the second bridge, suddenly all hell let loose, and I thought, My God, the leading company [Howard's] really has run into it, because there was tracer going off, explosions, flashes, bangs, goodness knows what. We discovered when we got to the bridge that in fact what had happened was that the leading company had shot up an old French tank that the Germans had been using and this was all the ammunition exploding....

Within less than an hour of our arrival, fairly heavy counterattacks started coming in, led by tanks of the 21st Panzer Division, and we had quite a sticky time — well, I should say a very sticky time for some people that night. I mean, A Company lost all its officers killed or wounded; they were whittled down to about fourteen men intact out of a company strength of normally about 120.

Also present — eventually — was Sergeant William French, who led a section in a machine-gun platoon. French remembered:

We weren't on the dropping zone.... I picked up one of my mates and eventually we found another one.... Just three of us had got together. I said, "We're too far south, we'd better go for the north." We hadn't been on the ground ten minutes and Jerry opened fire on us. We heard a tank go along the road and it must have seen us.... We found a sunken road...then we saw someone walking up the road toward us. We asked him for the password and he said, "Bloody hell, I've forgotten it." It was our platoon commander, so we soon put him in his place.

Parachuting into Normandy

Eric "Bill" Sykes (below), of the 7th (Light Infantry) Battalion, the Parachute Regiment, has never forgotten coming down about twenty miles or so from the intended drop zone:

"Once free of the aircraft, I found myself drifting across a moonlit road into an apple orchard.... For recognition purposes, we had been given a little tin gadget known as a 'cricket' [replica, below] which when pressed emitted a clicking sound. The drill was to click once and receive a couple of clicks in return, or vice-versa.... Now was the time for me to locate my partners in crime, the 'friendlies.' I clicked my cricket — nothing. I clicked again — nothing. One more try, and a voice which I assumed to be the voice of the platoon sergeant (a man of few, but mostly four-letter, words) boomed across the aisle between the apple trees: 'If the person who is doing that f*#&ing clicking doesn't shut up right now, I'm going to come over there and blow his bloody head off.' And that was a friendly!"

57

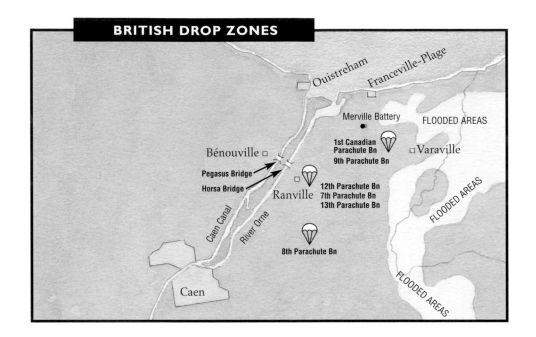

BRITISH DROP ZONES

Ouistreham
Franceville-Plage
Merville Battery
FLOODED AREAS
Bénouville
1st Canadian Parachute Bn
9th Parachute Bn
Varaville
Pegasus Bridge
Horsa Bridge
Ranville
12th Parachute Bn
7th Parachute Bn
13th Parachute Bn
FLOODED AREAS
Caen Canal
River Orne
8th Parachute Bn
FLOODED AREAS
Caen

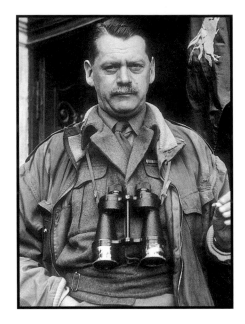

The 5th Brigade suffered almost one hundred casualties in the process of landing — broken bones, head injuries and the like — before firing a shot. Leaving the 7th Battalion to reinforce Howard, the 13th prepared a landing zone for the mass of gliders due within hours with reinforcements and heavier gear, including light tanks and field artillery.

The battalion's scout platoon brought an unusual item of equipment — a dog, which descended in its own tailor-made parachute — one of two dropped into Normandy. The animal, an Alsatian called Bing, had to be rescued from a tall tree that had snagged his canopy. The troops found him useful because he heard enemy gunfire and vehicles well before they did. And he proved able to guide his handler, Ken Bailey, through enemy lines in the confused night actions that followed the landing. Bing was awarded the "animal VC," the Dickin Medal of the People's Dispensary for Sick Animals. He was returned unharmed to his owner after the war.

The 13th Battalion helped capture Ranville — chosen as a main concentration area for the brigade — and the neighboring hamlet of Le Bas de Ranville. Among the reinforcing glider deliveries was Major General Richard Gale and his divisional headquarters, at 0330. To add to the considerable German confusion, thousands of undersized dummy paratroops were dropped in other areas, with built-in fireworks exploding as they descended.

The 3rd Parachute Brigade, made up of the 1st Canadian and two British parachute battalions (8th and 9th), landed in scattered fashion after its airborne formation was disrupted by evasive action against enemy antiaircraft fire. The men were further hampered by the large number of fields defensively flooded by the

(Above left) The British airborne forces were charged with protecting the eastern flank of the invasion beaches. (Above) Major General Richard Gale, commander of the British 6th Airborne Division, had decided that only gliders could pull off the critical element of surprise needed in the first hours of D-Day. (Below) Bing the Alsatian receives a congratulatory pat shortly after receiving the Dickin Medal (left), the "Victoria Cross" for animals.

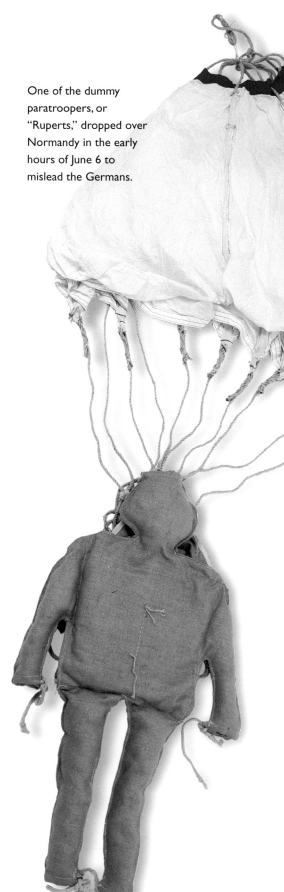

One of the dummy paratroopers, or "Ruperts," dropped over Normandy in the early hours of June 6 to mislead the Germans.

German garrison. They encountered far more of these than expected because many were masked from aerial reconnaissance by the vegetation that stood above the water level. Some men drowned, others had difficulty shedding their parachute harness; many lost their weapons and equipment. Yet others landed alone and had to flounder about, looking for comrades or an officer to tell them what to do. Many units needed hours to assemble a modicum of fighting strength.

The assignment of Lieutenant Colonel T. B. H. Otway's 9th Parachute Battalion was to capture the coastal battery of four guns at Merville, just east of the Orne estuary. Each gun had a casemate of thick concrete, and the battery was defended by two hundred men in an elaborately designed network of concrete-lined dugouts. Of three supporting gliders intended to land at the battery, one came down fairly close, a second was shot down by the Germans and the third landed too far away for its passengers to take part in the action. With nothing heavier than a machine gun and no proper communications equipment, Otway could muster only 150 men to attack the battery, but knew he could lose no more time waiting for the missing hundreds. He decided to improvise.

Those present were divided into four groups that stormed the gun positions. In the bitter fighting — often hand to hand — that followed amid the warren of sandbags, concrete and earthen fortifications, British casualties reached fifty percent; only a score of Germans were captured unwounded. Otway reported his success by firing a Véry light to alert reconnaissance aircraft. And, just to make sure, he also reported it by carrier pigeon. Someone remembered to tell the Royal Navy, which was primed to shell the battery should the army fail. But later on D-Day, the German 1716th Artillery Regiment used its remaining guns to bombard the ruined battery — to such effect that the British were forced to withdraw. Intelligence had overestimated the importance of the targeted battery. It turned out to consist of four old French 75-mm guns from the First World War.

The 8th Battalion meanwhile was under orders to destroy the Dives bridges at the same time as Major Howard moved to seize and save the pair east of Ranville. Major A. J. C. Roseveare, of the Royal Engineers, and his team of specialists were dropped with the paratroops to lay the charges. Undeterred by the fact that, on landing in a flooded area, Roseveare could find only a handful of paratroopers to cover him, he commandeered a medical jeep and its trailer and drove to the bridge at Troarn with half his remaining men and half his stock of explosive charges. He despatched the rest to tackle the other, smaller bridge downstream at Bures. Eluding the attention of the few dozen Germans alert enough to challenge their progress in an overloaded jeep heading toward the river, Roseveare and his tiny force laid their explosives and blew a hole in the center of the Troarn bridge. Less

traumatically, but no less effectively, his other section of Royal Engineers blew the bridge at Bures.

The 1st Canadian Parachute Battalion achieved its objective by blowing up another bridge over the Dives near Robehomme, a few miles downstream of the British targets. In all, five crossings of the Dives were destroyed, the Merville battery was knocked out and the two bridges over the Orne and the Caen Canal were secured — all according to plan.

The triumphant 6th Airborne Division shook off the disruption of so many disjointed landings and gathered its strength on the ridge between the Orne and Dives, ready to beat off enemy counterattacks against the eastern flank of the main landings by sea.

Parts of the German 21st Panzer Division's 125th Panzer-Grenadier (PG) Regiment tried to dislodge the 12th British Parachute Battalion in a thrust toward Ranville with artillery support. The 21st Division's history notes:

> *The fighting ebbed away. It had now become clear that with the available forces alone, a success here could no longer be achieved. The British paratroops were not going to let themselves be overthrown so easily.*

On the other side of the Orne, elements of the 192nd PG Regiment from the same division — the only armored formation Rommel had been allowed to deploy in forward positions — tried hard in counterattacks to dislodge the 7th Parachute Battalion at the two bridges but were beaten off with heavy losses after hard fighting that lasted much of the day:

> *The lack of success was a shock. We had not expected something like this. It had always been predicted that we would throw an attacker back into the sea at once.*

(Opposite) The heavily overgrown Merville battery as it looks today. British intelligence had overestimated its importance. In fact, its only weapons were four obsolete French artillery pieces. (Inset) After landing, these paratroopers from the 12th Parachute Battalion spent four days trying to link up with the rest of their unit.

Regrouping on the Ground

For Canadian Roger Charbonneau (above), the drop into Normandy was only his second jump. "[It] went well for me but not so for many of my comrades, who found themselves in flooded marshes and drowned there, not being able to release their equipment in time." After making it to the rendezvous point and mustering up a total of fifty-five men, Charbonneau's group headed south and managed to capture and destroy their targeted bridge.

Jan de Vries (right) of the 1st Canadian Parachute Battalion was not as lucky:

"As I made my way, I tried to figure out what went wrong [and] why I was alone in a place where I could not recognize any features we had studied in the transit camp. After eluding German patrols just before daylight I met three men from my platoon.... We continued together and finally arrived late in the day at our high ground defence position.... Out of the 120 men in C Company who were to carry out the objectives, only 35 landed on the drop zone. The rest were scattered like myself or captured or killed. Some straggled in for days if they had managed to evade the Germans.... The four of us cursed the pilot who had dropped us so far away when we were told of the battles that had taken place."

Champagne and Bagpipes

After bandaging a flesh wound on his thigh, nineteen-year-old paratrooper John Butler (above), of C Company, 7th Battalion (Light Infantry), the Parachute Regiment, entered the Café Gondrée near Pegasus Bridge on June 7 badly in need of a drink of water. (The café was being used as a regimental aid post.) Monsieur Gondrée, the proprietor, happily gave him champagne instead — after disappearing momentarily to fetch an armful of muddy bottles that had been buried in the floor of his cellar. Butler recalls:

"Just then one of the medics said he could hear the pipes so I went outside with several bottles of champagne.... As the pipes grew louder, round the corner came Brigadier Lord Lovat with a piper on one side and I presume his bodyguard on the other. He looked neither left nor right as he marched down the street as though he was strolling through his Scottish estate. He carried no weapon but instead carried his swagger cane."

SERGEANT FRENCH OF THE 7TH PARAS WAS ONE OF THE FIRST TO HEAR THAT THE DEFENDERS of the two captured bridges were about to be relieved, just as the Germans were gathering in a nearby wood for another heavy counterattack:

The first we heard were the [bag]pipes of the commandos, and then they marched across the bridge.... They looked as if they'd had a good day's march but they kept on and they looked quite cheerful. The piper marched across in front of Lord Lovat.

Pipe Major William Haskin Millin, then aged twenty, had been kept busy by his aristocratic Scottish commander. Lovat got him to stand in the bow and play his pipes over the Tannoy system of the landing ship, which was cheered to the echo as it sailed past to its position near the head of the vast convoy assembling off the Isle of Wight. "We were the first to set out because we were going to be the first to hit the beaches."

The only "weapon" he took into battle was his set of pipes, the bag covered in the Clan Fraser tartan of the Lovats. Millin wore a battle dress tunic over his Cameron-clan kilt and a green commando beret (commandos disdained helmets). He also carried the standard, heavy Bergen rucksack with his rations and personal gear:

When we landed, [the beach at Ouistreham] was under heavy fire and lots of people were being killed. I jumped off [into] the water and I started to play the pipes...with water waist-high, right up onto the beach, then I stopped, then I dashed off when I saw an exit.

Lovat's brigade of twenty-six hundred officers and men consisted of one French, one Royal Marine and three British army all-volunteer commando units with special training for assaults and operations behind enemy lines. When an officer reported the "ham and jam" message signaling Howard's success, Lovat said, "Give us a tune, piper." Millin played "The Road to the Isles" as the commandos headed south:

> *The whole thing was ridiculous [Millin recalled]. A paratroop sergeant clearly shared this view and shouted: "What the...hell are you playing at, you mad bastard? Every German in France knows we're here now!"*

After the six-mile march from the beach, the commandos were less than three minutes late for their rendezvous with the paratroops at Pegasus Bridge. "We had to nail down the left-hand flank," Lovat remembered. He expected to be withdrawn when infantry of the 50th (Northumbrian) Division came up from Sword later on June 6. In fact, the brigade remained in the line for eighty-three days without relief and took forty percent casualties. By then the Germans' last hope of rolling up the Allied bridgehead from its eastern flank was long gone. "With the airborne and the navy we managed to do it...with great difficulty," Lovat said. The eastern flank of the nascent bridgehead was secure.

(Opposite) Pipe Major William Haskin Millin, tartan-swathed bagpipes in hand, prepares to leave the landing craft in the waters off Sword Beach. (Above) Commandos from Lord Lovat's 1st Special Service Brigade near Ranville later on June 6, guarding the roads leading to Pegasus Bridge against German counterattacks. An abandoned Horsa glider stands nearby.

CHAPTER FIVE

Target: Ste-Mère-Eglise

"On the night we took off, I told Adam [Parsons, my co-pilot] that no matter what happened, even if he looked over at me and saw nothing but hamburger meat, he was to get our troops in and get them in accurately, and that I would do the same for him."

— Colonel Charles H. Young, CO, 439th Troop Carrier Group

NINETY MINUTES after their British colleagues began to descend on the eastern flank of the invasion zone on the Orne estuary, 13,500 American parachutists of the 82nd and 101st Airborne Divisions commenced the equivalent task some fifty miles to the west, focusing on the complicated estuary of the river Vire at the southeastern corner of the Cotentin Peninsula of Normandy. In recognition of the importance and difficulty of their task, General Eisenhower had decided to make a surprise visit to the 101st on the eve of the drop, at one of their bases in Berkshire, west of London.

Nearly all the American pathfinders went astray — thanks to a bank of cloud over the drop zone and then enemy antiaircraft fire, which forced the pilots of the C-47s of U.S. Army Air Force IX Troop Carrier Command to disperse or divert. Some pathfinders were even dropped into the sea. Eisenhower reported:

The American airborne forces…were faced with greater initial difficulties. Owing to the cloud and atmospheric conditions, the pathfinders failed to locate the exact areas fixed for the parachute drops, and the inexperience of some of the pilots led to wide dispersal of troops and supplies. The 6,600 parachute elements of 101st Division were scattered over an area twenty-five miles by fifteen miles in extent, and sixty percent of their equipment was lost in consequence….

The American airborne assault involved 1,662 aircraft — half carrying troops, half supplies — and 512 gliders. Over eight hundred C-47s transported the main combat forces, guided by a series of beacons across England and supplemented by Royal Navy vessels in the Channel. They were under strict orders to preserve radio silence. Squadron after squadron therefore received no warning of the cloud barrier as they flew into it at roughly 600 feet and 120 miles per hour.

(Above) Sporting a bazooka antitank gun among his gear, American paratrooper Corporal Louis E. Laird stands in the doorway of a C-47. (Insets) The shoulder patches of the two American airborne divisions — the famed Screaming Eagle of the 101st (bottom), and the 82nd "All American" (top). (Opposite) Suited up and ready to go, American paratroopers cross the Channel for Normandy.

Drop — and Go!

As a member of the 316th Troop Carrier Group, pilot Julian "Bud" Rice (above) and his co-pilot delivered twenty-one 82nd Airborne paratroopers to the Ste-Mère-Eglise drop zones:

"As we crossed the Cherbourg coastline, we flew directly into a dense land-fog. The plane on my right wing immediately vanished from sight. I climbed out wide and up 500 feet on instruments, then leveled and continued on course. Less than a minute later we broke through the fog. The black sky was a colorful but frightening display of tracers and black-grey flak bursts. I pushed down hard on the yoke and leveled out at the 600 ft jump altitude. As we passed over the west side of Ste-Mère-Eglise, I could see large fires burning in the town. I had to throttle-down and manhandle the controls to burn off the excess speed we had built up during the fast letdown. Settling in at a mushy jump speed of 110 MPH, we reached the DZ and I gave the green light jump signal. In a matter of seconds the troopers were out the door and into the black night below."

When the aircraft emerged from the clouds, their tight and tidy V-formations had disintegrated. And when they were lit up by searchlights and fired on from the ground, the pilots' evasive actions created even greater disruption. Instead of slowing down to release their stick, they accelerated out of danger. Instead of levelling off to help the jumpers, they climbed or dived — and they lost all sense of where they were. Most of the drops were, in effect, blind. The overall result was a chaotic series of uncoordinated landings by the hundreds of mostly terrified, often airsick, eighteen- to twenty-four-man sticks.

Furthermore, the Germans had used the waters of the river Merderet to flood much of the area precisely to hamper paratroops and gliders. The overall effect of these hazards was devastating. Between forty and fifty percent of the American airborne corps were lost — either gone astray, killed or injured in accidents, or killed or wounded by enemy fire. Virtually no major unit was both in the right place and fully manned for its allotted task, and most were seriously understrength. Very few radios survived the drop. Pathfinder Rolland Duff discovered, after setting up his guidance equipment, that:

> *Much of the drop zone was flooded with water two to four feet deep.... I could hear the men that had dropped into the water, their cries of anguish, cries for help. They were weighted down with equipment so that they had to struggle in the water to get out. In the deeper water some of them were drowned. It was really quite a harrowing experience, not only for them but for myself, knowing that the signal we were sending out was dropping them into inundated areas.*

Since the American paratroopers lacked the single, quick-release buckle of their British contemporaries, they had to loosen — even cut — five straps to get out of their harnesses. They were also more heavily laden with weapons and ammunition and weighted down by backpacks so huge that it was impossible to sit. In their aircraft the men knelt, leaning the packs on the seating. If they fell over on the ground, all but the strongest had to be helped back onto their feet. Nevertheless, the two divisional major generals — Matthew Ridgway of the 82nd and Maxwell Taylor of the 101st — boosted morale by jumping with their men, a higher risk for them because of their relatively advanced ages (forty-nine and forty-three, respectively).

The half-dozen initial objectives assigned to the American Airborne were more complicated and dispersed than those of the British. They included the bridges across the river Merderet, which flows roughly north-south to the west of the town of Ste-Mère-Eglise, and the little town itself — astride the road from Cherbourg to Bayeux, the most important in the area. Paratroops were also to seize the four designated exits from Utah, due east of Ste-Mère-Eglise, and the locks and crossings of the river Douve — into which the Merderet flows and which runs eastward across the Cotentin to the town of Carentan, southwest of the estuary.

(Right) The American drop zones were concentrated on either side of the town of Ste-Mère-Eglise. The 82nd Airborne, landing west of the town, would seize bridges across the river Merderet and take the town of Ste-Mère-Eglise itself. The 101st Airborne would land to the east. Its paratroops would secure the exits that the landing forces would need to get off Utah Beach. The commanding officers of the American airborne divisions were Major General Maxwell D. Taylor of the 101st (below) and Major General Matthew Ridgway of the 82nd (bottom).

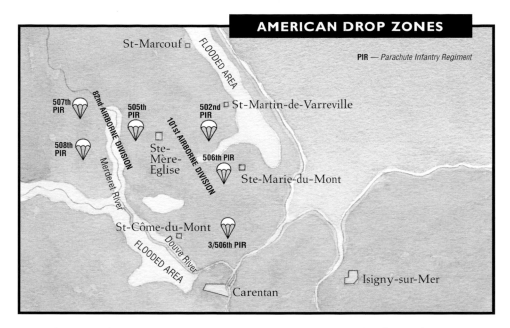

AMERICAN DROP ZONES

PIR — *Parachute Infantry Regiment*

St-Marcouf

FLOODED AREA

507th PIR

505th PIR

82nd AIRBORNE DIVISION

502nd PIR

St-Martin-de-Varreville

508th PIR

Ste-Mère-Eglise

101st AIRBORNE DIVISION

506th PIR

Ste-Marie-du-Mont

Merderet River

St-Côme-du-Mont

Douve River

3/506th PIR

FLOODED AREA

Carentan

Isigny-sur-Mer

The overriding purpose was to protect the western, or right, flank of the seaborne invasion from the Germans in Cherbourg and the Cotentin. The seizure of the various objectives was also intended to facilitate movement inland from Utah to the west and Omaha to the east of the Vire estuary by the seaborne troops, and subsequent communications between the forces from both beaches as they pressed inland.

Lieutenant Colonel Günther Keil of the 1058th Infantry Regiment (attached to the German 91st Airborne Division stationed around the Vire estuary, and the strongest in the Cotentin) recalled the chaos on the ground in the dark as several German units of various sizes and types milled about, trying to get a grip on an enemy who had no idea of his own strength on the ground or even of his whereabouts:

At 2400 hours [on June 5] enemy parachute troops made a jump over my command post by the quarry at Hill 69, north of the Quineville-Montebourg road [about six miles due north of Ste-Mère-Eglise]. The paratroops were taken prisoner. From the maps in [their] possession…it was evident that the main area for the drop would be Ste-Mère-Eglise…. At 0200 [messengers from two nearby battalions]…arrived at the regimental command post and reported that thousands of paratroops had jumped and their [own] units had been surrounded. Prior to then I had not regarded the situation as so serious because I believed that in this terrain of hedgerows, paratroops would have difficulty in orienting themselves and that some would even land in the wrong places, like those who had jumped near my command post though destined for Ste-Mère-Eglise. Furthermore, at first I did not believe that it was a question of a drop by complete divisions.

Setting down in France

David M. "Buck" Rogers (below, left) of the 101st Airborne recalls his landing:

"When my parachute opened…I knew without a doubt that I was directly over the church steeple [in Ste-Marie-du-Mont]. I drifted to the edge of the village and landed with my parachute caught in a small tree in a fencerow. I got out of my parachute and was looking around when I saw a shadowy figure about 150 feet along the fencerow moving toward me…. It was my battalion sergeant major, Sergeant Isaac Cole, and we were extremely happy to see each other. Before long, Sergeant Cole and I had gathered together six or seven other paratroopers, none of whom I knew. We didn't bother to ask their names or what unit they belonged to. We were just glad to have this small group together in one place."

Donald "Jake" Jakeway (below, right) of the 82nd Airborne spent ten days "playing hide and seek" with the Germans before he was reunited with his company:

"I floated downward and then landed in the branches of a tree in a small churchyard. I can tell you now, I was shook up…. I used my trench knife to cut free of my chute, dropped down and made a dash for the nearest hedgerow…. I waited for what seemed ages before I began to realize that I was alone, in Normandy, not knowing where anyone was."

(Left) As a buddy provides cover, a member of the 82nd Airborne storms the church at Ste-Mère-Eglise to take out a sniper. (Above) The church today bears very few scars from the fierce fighting that took place in and around it during the first hours of D-Day.

Confusion ensued among the Germans — compounded, ironically, by the initial disarray of the scattered Americans. The German forces in the western Cotentin included the 709th and 716th static Coastal Defense Divisions and parts of the 352nd Infantry Division. There was no major armored unit. Neither side realized, sometimes for several hours, what it was up against. Keil, for example, asked divisional headquarters for permission to send an army-reserve artillery unit from its position six miles to the north to attack Ste-Mère-Eglise as infantry. By the time its commanding major was ready and in position at noon on the sixth, it was too late. After much bloody fighting, the Americans of the 2nd and 3rd Battalions of the 505th Parachute Infantry Regiment had secured an unshakable grip on the town.

An Allied air raid had done some damage to Ste-Mère-Eglise, setting buildings on fire, before the paratroops began to drop. German soldiers helping with firefighting shot at the Americans as they appeared over the town center. A few dropped into the flames and died when their own ammunition blew up. Private John Steele was left dangling from the church tower for several hours when his canopy caught on one of the four finials. (Steele was eventually taken prisoner after the Germans realized he wasn't dead.) Strangely, after the Germans had doused the flames, they seemed to ignore the descent of the first three or four dozen American paratroopers and went back to bed.

An astonished Lieutenant Colonel Ed Krause, commanding the 3rd Battalion, had landed outside the village. He sent the men from his plane to gather up as many scattered Americans as they could quickly find. He then advanced quietly on the town, sealed all its exits and reached the central area around the church. He also cut the main enemy telephone cable from Cherbourg — an important contribution to German confusion — but he could not immediately report it because, like so many of his comrades, he had no radio.

Meanwhile, after his own landing, Lieutenant Colonel Ben Vandevoort quickly gathered the vast majority of the 630 men of his 2nd Battalion and advanced toward Ste-Mère-Eglise from the north — with a view to setting up a strong roadblock on the main highway, at the village of Neuville-au-Plain. Unfortunately he had fractured a leg on impact and had to be wheeled into action in a requisitioned farm cart. The regimental commander, Colonel Bill Ekman, lacking news of his 3rd Battalion, ordered the 2nd to advance into the town. Vandevoort moved on, leaving Lieutenant Turner Turnbull and a platoon astride the road at Neuville. Vandevoort passed through the town and set up a roadblock on the main highway to the south, just in time to fend off a determined attack by half a battalion of German infantry and a troop of tanks.

(Opposite) A replica paratrooper hangs today from one of the finials on the church spire in Ste-Mère-Eglise — commemorating the plight of American paratrooper Private John Steele, who survived after being snagged there amid enemy fire. It is also a lasting tribute from grateful parishioners to the American troops who descended from the skies in the early hours of June 6, 1944.

On Double Duty

Eighteen-year-old Robert Murphy (above) of the 1st Battalion, the 505th Parachute Infantry Regiment, 82nd Airborne Division, had been handpicked as a pathfinder:

"Three men from each company…had double duty to train as infantrymen but also jump ahead as pathfinders (top) with lights and radar/radio beacons. Finishing that job, we returned to fight with our regular unit…. The sole D-Day mission of Company A 505 was to seize and hold the La Fière bridge that spans the road west of Ste-Mère-Eglise and runs over the Merderet River."

Murphy and his unit made a heroic stand at the river crossing — taking the bridge on June 6 and holding it for three days until relief arrived. "No German crossed it again, except as a prisoner of war."

The Kindness of Strangers

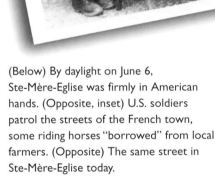

Nine-year-old Marie-Thérèse Champel (standing beside her sister and brothers in the photo, below right) awoke with a start around 6 A.M. on June 6, 1944. From her bedroom on an isolated farm near the village of Prétot in the heart of the Cotentin, she could hear a commotion and unfamiliar voices in the house. She quickly raced to investigate:

"A strange man sat on a chair in the middle of our kitchen. He wore a sort of khaki uniform with pockets everywhere. His helmet was covered with foliage and his face was smeared black. He spoke incomprehensible words. My mother and my brothers tried to speak with him. He cradled his arm and kept repeating 'broken…broken.' Suddenly he reached to the bottom of his pant leg, cut a fabric band there and took out — wonder! — a chocolate bar that he offered to us."

The stranger turned out to be American paratrooper Warren Shaw of the 82nd Airborne, who had broken his shoulder when he landed near the Champel property. He was later hidden from the Germans at a Champel relative's farm while he recovered from his injuries (top right).

At the same time, Turnbull came under attack from a company of the 1058th Regiment, supported by at least two armored vehicles. The Germans were nonchalantly singing as they marched southward down the highway but responded like veterans when the Americans opened fire, taking cover and shooting back. Turnbull, outnumbered by five to one and heavily outgunned, held out for eight vital hours until he slipped away with less than half of his platoon — only to die in action the next day.

But Ste-Mère-Eglise, the key to the airborne operation, was securely in American hands. Many other isolated but bitter little battles took place in the marshy southeast corner of the Cotentin — some won by the paratroops, some by the Germans. Small, spontaneously formed groups of Americans secured major objectives while larger units never even managed to assemble for an attack. Many officers found themselves in more or less the right place, but without many — or sometimes any — men to command. One such officer was General Taylor of the 101st Airborne, who eventually led a company-sized scratch force of "brass" and noncombatants in an attack on a strategically important village and found time to parody Winston Churchill: "Never in the history of human conflict have so few been led by so many." But the defenders could not neutralize, still less reverse, the airborne attack, however uneven and disrupted or wasteful of manpower. Bedeviled by poor, or nonexistent, communications, the U.S. airborne corps nevertheless managed to gain its main objective — a sufficiently secure airhead in the hinterland of Utah Beach. The overture was complete. The first act could now begin.

(Below) By daylight on June 6, Ste-Mère-Eglise was firmly in American hands. (Opposite, inset) U.S. soldiers patrol the streets of the French town, some riding horses "borrowed" from local farmers. (Opposite) The same street in Ste-Mère-Eglise today.

CHAPTER SIX

The Sea and Air Assault

"As we neared the beaches at approximately 2 A.M., the skies were ablaze with fire and antiaircraft fire. It looked like hell on earth. Gasoline dumps were going up, hit by terrific bombing by the Allies."

— Radio operator Ed Black, aboard destroyer escort USS *Rich* early on June 6

AS BRITISH AND AMERICAN PARATROOPS fought for the first footholds in Normandy, the Allied air forces launched a massive preparatory bombardment. They had been attacking coastal defenses and transport facilities in France for many weeks (at a cost of some twelve thousand airmen and two thousand aircraft in two months). Now they targeted the Wehrmacht installations that were most likely to present an immediate threat to the seaborne troops as they landed — especially gun batteries and coastal strongpoints. But the ocean of concrete the Germans had poured into their "Atlantic Wall" ensured that even direct hits by massive bombs or the heaviest naval guns usually failed to destroy them.

Between 3 A.M. and 5 A.M. on D-Day, more than one thousand RAF high-level bombers released a horrific five thousand tons of bombs on the coastal defenses in the British sector, east of Bayeux. As first light and H-Hour — the moment of landing — approached, the U.S. 8th Air Force sent twelve hundred high-level, heavy bombers to support the RAF and also strike the area west of Bayeux (around Omaha Beach). The heavy bombers were frustrated by the same low cloud bank that had made life difficult for the American airborne troops. In fact, many U.S. bombers returned to England with an undropped load. Those who attacked dropped their bombs by timetable, but the cloud caused widespread disruption and also forced them to bomb blind.

(Left) U.S. Army Air Force B-26 bombers, their wings marked with the distinctive stripes painted on all invasion aircraft, roar over the fleet. Of the 742 B-26s that took to the skies on June 6, only six of the aircraft were reported missing in action.

Many pilots, understandably anxious to avoid hitting the first wave of landing troops, delayed release by a few seconds. As every second's delay took the aircraft some four hundred feet farther, many bombs — especially at Omaha — exploded noisily behind the beach without affecting the defenses. This was just one of several American "pulled punches" at Omaha that helped make it the deadliest beach on D-Day. The 9th Air Force, however, successfully unleashed its medium bombers on the southwest corner of the Cotentin, the Utah area, from a few hundred feet, below the clouds — the perfect action in the circumstances.

(Above left) B-26s bomb targets in northern France. (Above right) Bomber crews of the U.S. 9th Air Force leave their B-26 Marauder aircraft after returning from a successful raid on German supply and communications lines.

Cleaning Up Utah Beach

As bomber pilot Harvey A. Jacobs (right), of the 9th Air Force, 497th Bomb Squadron, headed his B-26 toward the Normandy coast, his orders were clear:

"Our targets were the gun emplacements at Utah, specifically La Madeleine, Beau Guillot and St-Martin-de-Varreville.... We were to start all bombing operations at H-Hour minus 20 — and every two minutes thereafter, another wave of bombers would send their regards whistling down to the enemy below.... The weather that morning was horrendous, the worst in over one hundred years. We could not reach our normal flight altitude, so in essence, we went in at low level. As I was flying on my flight leader's left wing, I was the fifteenth plane over Utah on that day. Our box of thirty-six planes had St.-Martin-de-Varreville as our assigned target — and after dropping our load of destruction at precisely 0609 hours, we headed toward England.... [On our way back] we were caught in a murderous cross fire of flak...."

(Above) In this watercolor by Dwight Shepler, Canadian Minesweeping Squadron 31, supported by U.S. destroyers *Emmons* and *Doyle*, clears a bombardment support lane to the Normandy coast during the night before H-Hour. In the distance, the green and red markers dropped by pathfinders add an eerie light to the cloud-covered sky — as does the opening of the air attack on Pointe du Hoc.

JUST AS THE EFFORTS OF EACH NATIONAL AIR FORCE WERE FOCUSED — THOUGH NOT EXCLUSIVELY — on helping its own troops until the last minute before landing, so the two navies usually provided the seaborne support for their own armies. The Royal Navy and Royal Canadian Navy supplied the bulk of the general cover — including antisubmarine patrols, minesweepers, convoy escorts, support and bombardment ships. As planned, the U.S. Army attacked on the right, or western, side of the front from its bases in southwestern England, with close support provided by the U.S. Navy. Admiral Ramsay had organized his ships accordingly, into an Eastern (British) Task Force under Rear Admiral Sir Philip Vian, and a Western one under Rear Admiral A. G. Kirk, USN. An assault force was assigned to each beach: Forces U (Utah) and O (Omaha) were American; G (Gold), J (Juno) and S (Sword) were British and Canadian. Each of these had the support of a shore-bombardment group, and each Allied navy provided a flotilla for its own follow-up forces — the troops that would be landed over the beaches after D-Day (the U.S. deployed Force B; the British, Force L). Each beach was assigned a naval captain of the appropriate nationality to take charge ashore.

THE GERMANS HAD NO CHANCE OF FINDING AN EFFECTIVE COUNTER AGAINST THE OVERWHELM-ingly superior Allied air and naval forces. Like the Luftwaffe, the Kriegsmarine was but a shadow of what it had been in the early years of the war. All German capital warships had been sunk or driven from the seas, and in spring 1943 the Anglo-Canadians had at last largely defeated the U-boat menace after vast mercantile shipping losses. But the Slapton disaster was a reminder that the German navy, though down, was not out. The twenty-two U-boats stationed in Norway stayed put because they lacked the "snorkel" breathing tube without which they could not hope to evade the Allied antisubmarine sea and air patrols. Of the thirty-six in the occupied Brittany ports, only nine had snorkels; of the seventeen in the North Atlantic in June 1944, only ten were equipped with them.

The Germans assembled a scratch force of thirty-five submarines against the Allied invasion fleet. Two were sunk and eight damaged in the first twenty-four hours of the invasion; three were sunk the next day. The U-boats achieved nothing until June 15, when they sank a British destroyer and an American tank-landing ship. Of the half-dozen enemy destroyers still afloat in French waters, the Royal Navy sank two and damaged two; the others were under repair and did not emerge. The most effective German effort at sea, apart from some lethal mining, was made by the nearly fifty E-boats and smaller torpedo boats. In the first week of the invasion, they sank or disabled twenty smaller Allied vessels. RAF Bomber Command made a rare departure from its nocturnal routine to bomb the E-boat pens in the Pas de Calais — its biggest daylight raid of the war, executed by nearly 350 bombers. Many boats were damaged, and most of them took little further part in the war.

The Luftwaffe now had fewer than 350 aircraft in France — nowhere near enough to deploy effectively against the opposition it faced. Most of the German bomber squadrons had been sent to the eastern front long since, while dwindling fighter forces were concentrated against the Allied bombing of Germany. So the Luftwaffe put its effort into sowing mines at sea — a constant nuisance until August. The latest German "Oyster" mines, made in both acoustic and magnetic versions, were difficult to dispose of, and the Allied minesweeper force initially could barely keep up with the threat.

ON JUNE 4, THE FIVE COMPONENTS OF THE INVASION ARMADA GATHERED FROM THEIR MANY ports in southern England in an "Area Z" southeast of the Isle of Wight. The waters of the Solent between the island and the mainland had swarmed with nearly a thousand ships since April. Mock "troop movements" northward up the east coast at the beginning of June sought to sustain the mythical threat to Norway, while dummy ships in the Dover area kept the Pas de Calais notion alive. The Admiralty chart of Area Z and the southward routes from it to the five beaches looks like the rose of a watering can in full flood (it was nicknamed the "spray can" by staff officers). Sea conditions were choppy to rough with waves of up to six feet on the eve of the landing — postponed as it was from the fifth to the sixth.

As far as could be determined in advance, tidal conditions on the fifth were, on paper, ideal; the sixth was second-best. The tide comes in from the broad Atlantic from west to east up the Channel, rising twenty-four feet at a rate of about five feet per hour. The optimum moment for landing was three to four hours before high tide, so that obstacles could be demolished and the landing craft could be carried on the tide as close as possible — with enough time to go back for more troops without grounding. This meant that the Americans would be going ashore up to an hour before the British and that the landings would begin in daylight.

The Night before the Invasion

Robert A. York (below) was a gunner's mate third class on the Coast Guard vessel USS *Bayfield*. After engaging in amphibious maneuvers off England and Scotland for four months, the *Bayfield* departed for the invasion of France on June 5 as the flagship of Rear Admiral D. P. Moon. The armada grew as more and more ships joined the southbound convoy. York and another mate were in charge of placing detonating rockets on the *Bayfield*'s rocket boats. On the night before the invasion, York worked until about 10 P.M. and then went to the mess hall to join the many crewmembers already there:

"To stay awake, we were drinking coffee so black it could float a spoon.… The heartburn was so bad that come daylight, when the actual invasion began, we thought it would be a relief to get killed on the beach.… Of course, we talked like this because we were so young and naive."

"I picked up my artillery binoculars and stepped back with amazement when I saw that the horizon was literally filling with ships of all kinds. It seemed impossible to me that this vast fleet could have gathered without anyone being the wiser."

— Major Werner Pluskat, from a bunker overlooking Omaha Beach at dawn on June 6

(Below) By dusk on June 5, the sea off the coast of England had become a vast armada of ships waiting to sail toward the Normandy coast. (Insets, left and middle) Protected by barrage balloons overhead, a convoy of invasion craft moves across the English Channel. (Inset, right) A lookout on the HMCS *Prince David* watches as assault craft head toward the beaches of Normandy.

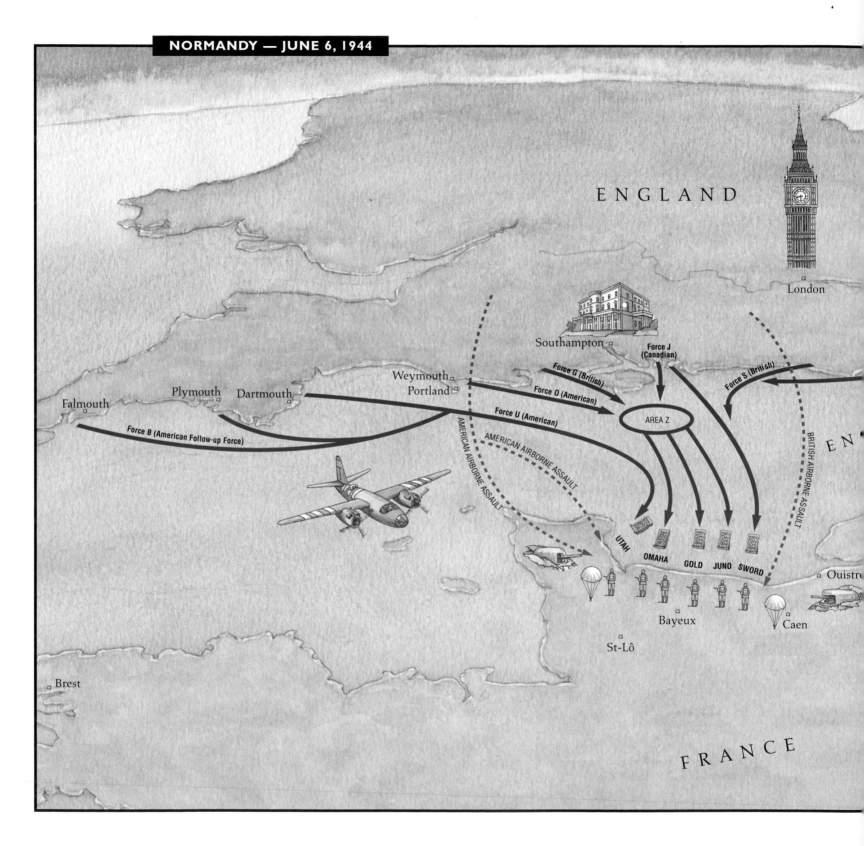

ENGLAND

London

Southampton

Force J
(Canadian)

Weymouth
Portland

Force G (British)

Force O (American)

Force S (British)

Falmouth

Plymouth   Dartmouth

Force U (American)

AREA Z

EN

Force B (American Follow-up Force)

AMERICAN AIRBORNE ASSAULT

AMERICAN AIRBORNE ASSAULT

BRITISH AIRBORNE ASSAULT

UTAH

OMAHA   GOLD   JUNO   SWORD

Ouistre

Bayeux

Caen

St-Lô

Brest

FRANCE

Force L (British Follow-up Force)

elixstowe

arwich

H CHANNEL

Calais

Boulogne

Dieppe

The Largest Convoy Ever Assembled

Seaman Edwin Black (below, and in doorway in photo at right) was a radioman aboard the USS *Rich* and was also the trainer on the 1.1-inch antiaircraft guns. On June 2, the *Rich* received word that it was to participate in the invasion as escort ship for the battleship USS *Nevada*:

"We loaded ammunition just out of Londonderry, so much we could hardly walk in the passageways…. Docking in Plymouth…there were LSTs, troop transports, all types of navy craft. Extra guns were placed on the Rich…. On June 5, with the invasion postponed for a day, we just stayed in the Channel in the largest convoy ever assembled…all types of men of war. We had barrage balloons tied above the ships to keep German aircraft away."

On June 8, the *Rich* sank after hitting mines off Utah Beach. Miraculously, Edwin Black survived.

THE INVASION FLEET THAT GATHERED ON THE NIGHT OF JUNE 4 AND MOVED SOUTHWARD ACROSS the western end of the Channel on the fifth was the greatest ever brought together. Thousands of landing ships, cargo ships and all manner of specialized vessels moved majestically forward in unison — surrounded by destroyers and frigates, interspersed with antiaircraft ships and preceded by the heavily escorted bombardment ships. A few German sentinels saw it from their observation posts on the beaches of Normandy and could not believe their eyes. The superiors to whom they breathlessly reported (before the Resistance brought down so many telephone wires) usually did not believe them and took no action.

(Opposite) Getting the troops to the beaches of Normandy on June 6, 1944, was a masterpiece of sea-going traffic control. American forces from the west joined up with the fleets carrying British and Canadian soldiers in a zone south of the Isle of Wight known as Area Z. The parachute forces secured the flanks of the invasion beaches by night, and then the Allied fleets headed for France along a series of channels swept clear of mines. Behind them sailed the follow-up naval forces B and L.

Lieutenant James West Thompson, USN, was stores officer aboard an LST (Landing Ship, Tank) in Plymouth, Devon:

The LST-505 loaded up several days before the invasion at Plymouth, England.... We took about 445 officers and men and spent a number of days in this crowded condition.... Living conditions aboard ship were not at all happy. Our tank deck and main deck were both filled with various trucks and motor vehicles but did not include any tanks. Finally on June 4 we set out for the landing in France. The weather was heavily overcast and the seas rather rough and we had not proceeded far before we received orders to return to port at Plymouth. There we waited until the next day, when we again set out on the same course to the east. During the night we turned south toward the French coast, and I can remember making out the Cotentin Peninsula in the dim light, off to our starboard.

Derek Knight was deputy head of the British army's Film and Photographic Unit and was in the vanguard of this extraordinary display of naval might:

When the first light came up, we were surrounded by this tremendous armada of ships. Close by there was a PLUTO (Pipe Line Under The Ocean) ship. There were the ships towing the Mulberry harbors, there were the attack ships, and most of all there were these rocket ships, which were the most frightening things. They had hundreds of rockets on the deck, and when we got off the shore of Normandy these things fired off. It was like a...[fireworks display] on a grand scale — tremendous numbers of rockets being poured onto the beachhead, and this was backed up by the battleships.... They were bombarding the beaches, ready for us to go ashore.

IN THE LAST PHASE OF THE ALLIED BOMBERS' PRE-LANDING RAIDS, THE WARSHIPS (BATTLESHIPS, monitors, cruisers, destroyers) joined in the preliminary bombardment with a carefully orchestrated pounding of shore targets — sometimes only yards ahead of the invading troops, occasionally even in their midst. These 174 bombardment ships remained on call for specific tasks as long as their guns, with ranges of up to twenty-two miles in the biggest ships, could help the troops on the ground. Naval officers went ashore to register the fall of shot and to direct fire. Spotter planes flew overhead for the same purposes.

On June 5, Admiral Ramsay wrote in his neatly penciled handwriting in the diary he kept (against regulations) throughout the war:

I am under no delusion as to the risks involved in this most difficult of all operations.... We shall require all the help that God can give us and I cannot believe that this will not be forthcoming.

General Eisenhower addressed the 285,000 sailors, 660,000 airmen and nearly two million troops of his command:

You are about to embark upon the Great Crusade.... The eyes of the world are upon you.... In company with our brave Allies and brothers-in-arms on other Fronts, you will bring about the destruction of the German war machine [and] the elimination of Nazi tyranny.... Your task will not be an easy one. Your enemy is well trained, well equipped and battle-hardened.... We will accept nothing less than full Victory! Good Luck! And let us all beseech the blessing of Almighty God upon this great and noble undertaking.

In the wallet of the supreme commander, Allied Expeditionary Force, however, was secreted the following note, dated June 5:

Our landings in the Cherbourg-Havre area have failed to gain a satisfactory foothold and I have withdrawn the troops. My decision to attack at this time and place was based upon the best information available. The troops, the air and the navy did all that bravery and devotion to duty could do. If any blame or fault attaches to the attempt, it is mine alone.

Eisenhower would never come closer to needing this slip of paper than in the first hours of battle on a French beach incongruously code-named "Omaha."

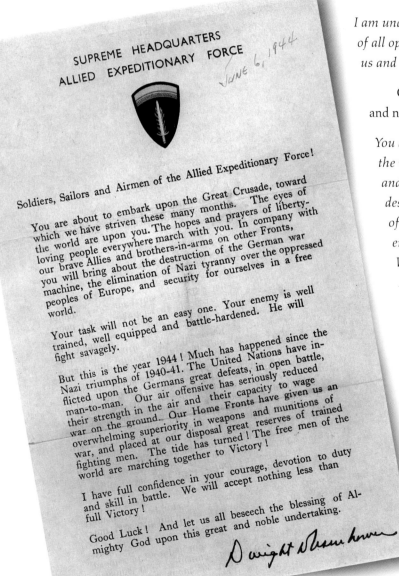

SUPREME HEADQUARTERS
ALLIED EXPEDITIONARY FORCE

June 6, 1944

Soldiers, Sailors and Airmen of the Allied Expeditionary Force!

You are about to embark upon the Great Crusade, toward which we have striven these many months. The eyes of the world are upon you. The hopes and prayers of liberty-loving people everywhere march with you. In company with our brave Allies and brothers-in-arms on other Fronts, you will bring about the destruction of the German war machine, the elimination of Nazi tyranny over the oppressed peoples of Europe, and security for ourselves in a free world.

Your task will not be an easy one. Your enemy is well trained, well equipped and battle-hardened. He will fight savagely.

But this is the year 1944! Much has happened since the Nazi triumphs of 1940-41. The United Nations have inflicted upon the Germans great defeats, in open battle, man-to-man. Our air offensive has seriously reduced their strength in the air and their capacity to wage war on the ground. Our Home Fronts have given us an overwhelming superiority in weapons and munitions of war, and placed at our disposal great reserves of trained fighting men. The tide has turned! The free men of the world are marching together to Victory!

I have full confidence in your courage, devotion to duty and skill in battle. We will accept nothing less than full Victory!

Good Luck! And let us all beseech the blessing of Almighty God upon this great and noble undertaking.

Dwight Eisenhower

CHAPTER SEVEN

Utah and Bloody Omaha

"At 5:50 A.M., [the *Augusta*] shuddered as it opened fire upon its predesignated targets among the beach defenses. The salvo coasted over the armada and we followed the pinpoints of light as they plunged down toward the shore."

— Lieutenant General Omar N. Bradley, aboard the invasion flagship *Augusta*, off Omaha Beach on June 6

■ THE LONG COASTLINE OF NORMANDY that faces northward to England, between the Cotentin Peninsula to the west and Le Havre to the east, consists of wide, sandy beaches between often extensive outcrops of rock, and river estuaries with sandbanks and mudflats visible only at low tide. The five landing beaches were spaced out along a stretch of coastline some forty-four miles long. The golden sands look most attractive; were the Norman climate warmer and more reliable, they would be swarming with tourists in summer. As it is, they were popular for day trips before the war, as they remain today. They shelve gently and evenly, which means that the incoming tide rapidly reduces the area of dry sand between the generally low, grassy dunes of the coastline and the sea. The band of shingle a few yards wide — well nigh impassable to pedestrians and vehicles alike — that lay immediately in front of the dunes in 1944 has disappeared in most places since the war. But there is still a strip of soft, dry sand inland of the firm, tidal area.

Utah Beach is at the "corner" where the coastline turns northward to form the eastern side of Cotentin. In fact, it faces northeast by east and is at the southern end of a long and particularly broad, sandy coastline. The dunes are low here and the land behind them flat — all reminiscent of the Belgian and Dutch coasts. In many ways this was the "easiest" of the five chosen landing areas, exacting the fewest casualties. There were four exits — all minor roads or tracks at right angles to the beach — leading through the dunes onto firm land, and a minor highway running parallel to the beach about three miles inland.

Omaha, by contrast, was undoubtedly the most difficult invasion beach in physical terms as well as military. Though offering a broad enough sweep of sand at low tide (as much as a quarter of a mile), there are only a few yards left when the tide comes in. Situated between the river Douve estuary and the vertical stone cliff some two hundred feet high at Pointe du Hoc, both to the west, and the rocky coastline on either side of Port-en-Bessin to the east, it is a little over six miles wide.

What distinguishes it from the other invasion beaches is the near-vertical bluff or bank — the leading edge of a plateau up to 150 feet high, ten miles wide and up to two miles deep — that stands a few dozen yards inland of the beach. Men could scramble up it but not vehicles, and when they reached the top they found convoluted, even tortuous, terrain that was ideal for concealment. As Omaha was the only large beach on a twenty-five-mile stretch of coastline, the Germans had prepared particularly strong defenses — digging an antitank ditch between the bluff and the road along the beach, while lavishing concrete on strongpoints. In 1944, the western third of the beach, where the bluff petered out, was protected behind the shingle by a seawall of wood and stone (since demolished). There were four exits — all small roadways that ran southward for up to a mile to the minor highway running behind the beach and Pointe du Hoc along the coast from Port-en-Bessin toward Isigny-sur-Mer to the southwest.

(Top) American soldiers on board a large LSI (Landing Ship, Infantry) wait silently for their turn to hit the invasion beaches. These larger craft were just one of the many types carrying the invasion force ashore. Smaller landing craft (above) transported the first waves of assault troops. (Opposite) The American beaches.

(Previous page) Omaha Beach today. (Inset) Smoke pours from an incoming landing craft at Omaha Beach moments after it was hit by German machine-gun fire on June 6, 1944. Amazingly, the boat's coxswain made it to the beach, landed his troops and returned to his ship.

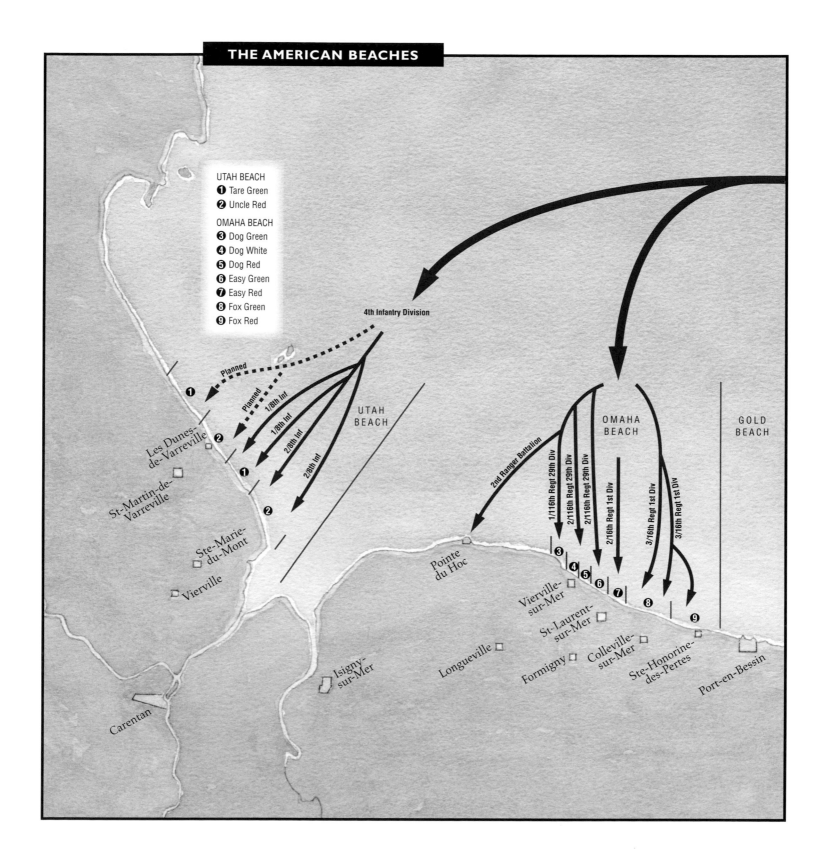

UTAH BEACH
❶ Tare Green
❷ Uncle Red

OMAHA BEACH
❸ Dog Green
❹ Dog White
❺ Dog Red
❻ Easy Green
❼ Easy Red
❽ Fox Green
❾ Fox Red

4th Infantry Division

Planned

Planned

1/8th Inf

1/8th Inf

2/8th Inf

2/8th Inf

UTAH BEACH

2nd Ranger Battalion

1/116th Regt 29th Div

2/116th Regt 29th Div

2/116th Regt 29th Div

2/16th Regt 1st Div

3/16th Regt 1st Div

3/16th Regt 1st Div

OMAHA BEACH

GOLD BEACH

Les Dunes-de-Varreville

St-Martin-de-Varreville

Ste-Marie-du-Mont

Vierville

Pointe du Hoc

Vierville-sur-Mer

St-Laurent-sur-Mer

Colleville-sur-Mer

Ste-Honorine-des-Pertes

Port-en-Bessin

Isigny-sur-Mer

Longueville

Formigny

Carentan

THE ASSAULT FORCE ASSIGNED TO UTAH, THE WESTERNMOST BEACH — AND THEREFORE FIRST to be attacked — was the 4th Infantry Division of the United States Army, commanded by Major General Raymond O. Barton, spearhead of Major General J. Lawton Collins's VII Corps. The bombers had been and gone, and the sixteen bombardment ships of Naval Force A had just ceased fire. The plan was for eight LCTs (Landing Craft, Tank) with a total of thirty-two duplex-drive tanks to go in at 0630. They were to be followed immediately by the division's 8th Regimental Combat Team in two waves — the 2nd Battalion and then the 1st — supported by combat engineers, more tanks and armored bulldozers. But, as so often happens with the best-laid plans, it went awry.

As the fast-rising, incoming Atlantic tide peaks from west to east in the Channel, a strong current runs in the same direction offshore. Locally the current runs roughly from north to south off the east-facing Utah Beach. The LCTs, LCIs and especially the smaller, boxlike LCAs (Landing Craft, Assault) were easily diverted by the combination of a six-foot swell, choppy seas, a northerly wind and the current, in which they lurched and heaved uncomfortably. Many who had managed to avoid seasickness on the ships succumbed to it in the landing craft. The detailed timetable for the landings of the various craft was soon in tatters, with some arriving early and others late. Several command craft

(Opposite) Although the assault on Utah was the most straightforward of the five beaches, the troops still had to contend with German shells and mortars, as shown in a watercolor by Mitchell Jamieson (inset, left). The seawall (inset, right) provided cover and safety. (Bottom) Soldiers drag ashore survivors from a sunken landing craft. The waters off Utah were littered with mines and obstacles.

Rough Landing at Utah

Combat medic Jack Fox (top), with the 1st Battalion, 8th Infantry Regiment, 4th U.S. Infantry Division, landed at Utah Beach amid heavy fire from German shore batteries:

"I remember the bullets flying over our craft and seeing the ricochets of the bullets hitting the water. The landing craft's door fell open and we all ran into the surf. We were in very deep water and I thought I was either going to drown or be shot before getting to land. By the grace of God, I made it ashore and started running through the deep sand toward the seawall. I had saved my medical equipment and stopped to help a wounded soldier lying on the beach. I turned him over and realized he was dead. I recognized him as a friend of mine. I was shocked, scared and angry at the same time."

Fox has an autographed French bank note (right) that he keeps as a remembrance of his comrade-in-arms who never made it home:

"We had been issued 'invasion currency' that consisted of two 100-franc bank notes each. I lost one of the bank notes playing poker. I had some of my buddies sign the other bank note. Later, I managed to get autographs from Ernie Pyle and Ernest Hemingway, who were also coming ashore with us. I carried that autographed bank note throughout the war…. I plan on leaving it to my heirs."

"**The noise of the shelling was deafening. The smell of sulfur, vomit and fear was permeating. I was just praying that I would not die until I was on land....**"
— Combat medic Jack Fox, aboard an invasion landing craft on June 6

"All the way up and down the broad beach as far as I could see, men, jeeps, bulldozers and other equipment were moving about like ants."

— *Los Angeles Times* war correspondent Tom Treanor, reporting from Utah Beach on June 6

were also sunk by mines. (There were more German mines off Utah than any other beach; they eventually sank four destroyers and two minesweepers as well as smaller craft.) And to make matters even worse, the majority of the landing craft came ashore as much as two-thirds of a mile south of the targeted area.

Company E of the 2nd Battalion became the first seaborne infantry unit to land in Normandy, having overtaken the DD tanks that were supposed to protect them as they went ashore (the tanks had fallen behind the slightly faster LCAs in the heavy swell). With Company E was the deputy divisional commander, Brigadier General Theodore Roosevelt, Jr., son of the late American president of the same name and a distant cousin of the wartime leader. General Roosevelt had insisted on leading the landing from the front. Without a helmet, and swinging a walking stick, Roosevelt placed his faith in his own initiative. Instead of trying to correct the landing errors, he and Colonel James Van Fleet, the regimental commander, rallied the incoming troops and tanks and took them inland — thus by benign accident outflanking the strongest local defenses to the north of the erroneous landing zone. "We'll start the war from right here," Roosevelt declared. (He won the Congressional Medal of Honor for his leadership and coolness under fire at Utah.)

Utah turned out to be the most straightforward beach of the five, with fewer than two hundred casualties (dead, wounded or missing). The 4th Division pushed inland and soon linked up with men of the 101st Airborne, in time to repel counterattacks by parts of the 91st, 243rd and 709th German Divisions. The right flank was now nailed down, and follow-up forces with tanks and other vehicles poured across the broad sands of Utah in comparative safety. The Luftwaffe had hardly been heard from.

LST-505 LEFT THE COTENTIN TO STARBOARD AND TURNED EAST TOWARD OMAHA BEACH ON D-Day morning. Lieutenant Thompson recalled:

> *We anchored about two and a half or three miles offshore. We located our position as off Colleville-sur-Mer [behind the eastern end of the beach] by being able to see the steeple of the village church there. We could tell that a lot was going on ashore.... We were at General Quarters when we arrived.... I remember looking over the side of the ship and seeing several bodies pass by close to the ship. One was a young sailor whose hair was long enough to be streaming back in the water. The whole thing took on an air of grim reality.... We could see explosions on the beach, and we could see smoke rising from various sites.... We could see many small ships and craft in the water just offshore, some under way and others obviously wrecked.*

(Opposite) The flat sands of Utah Beach today and (inset) as they looked on June 6, 1944. Because of a series of lucky flukes, the American forces landed east of the heaviest beach defenses — making it possible for soldiers, including these men from the 4th Infantry Division (top), to wade ashore in relative safety. (Above) Every American soldier participating in the landings was issued an inflatable lifebelt. One of these (below) washed up on the invasion beaches after more than five decades underwater.

Since few photographers landed in the early waves of the assault, images such as these showing the American 16th Infantry Regiment landing at Omaha (below and opposite) are relatively rare.

THE LIEUTENANT WAS NOT DECEIVED. AS JUNE 6 WORE ON, THE SITUATION ON OMAHA, FIFTEEN miles east of Utah, became so fraught that General Bradley, commanding the U.S. 1st Army, seriously considered calling off the attack by his V Corps (Major General Leonard T. Gerow) — even though there could be no question of evacuating more than a fraction of those ashore, if any.

The main assault on Omaha was assigned to the U.S. 1st Infantry Division under Major General Clarence R. Huebner, supported by the 116th Infantry Regiment of the 29th Division, which went in on the western flank of the 1st Division's 16th Infantry Regiment.

The "pulled punch" of the American bombers, which delayed their bomb-drops by seconds for fear of hitting their own troops, had missed the formidable German shore defenses immediately behind the beach by as much as eleven hundred yards. Whole minefields, untouched in the smooth sands of the beach, lay in wait for the invaders. Now, apparently, it was the U.S. Navy's turn to exercise too much caution.

"As our boat touched sand and the ramp went down, I became a visitor to hell. "
— Private Harry Parley, E Company, 2nd Battalion, 116th Infantry Regiment

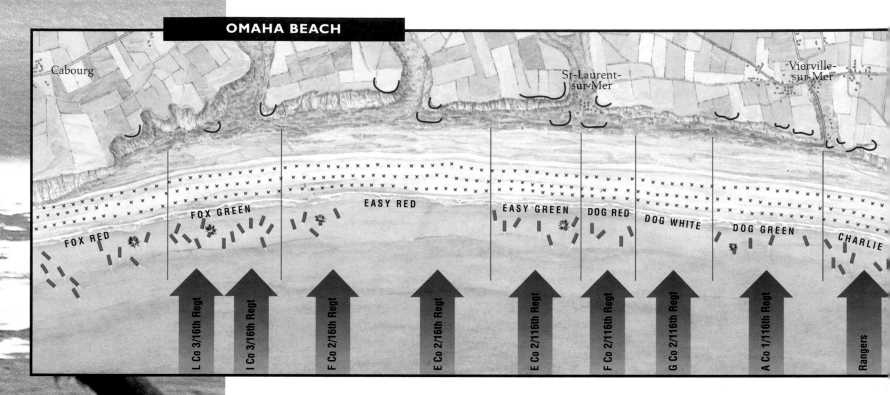

OMAHA BEACH

Cabourg

St-Laurent-sur-Mer

Vierville-sur-Mer

FOX RED

FOX GREEN

EASY RED

EASY GREEN

DOG RED

DOG WHITE

DOG GREEN

CHARLIE

L Co 3/16th Regt

I Co 3/16th Regt

F Co 2/16th Regt

E Co 2/16th Regt

E Co 2/116th Regt

F Co 2/116th Regt

G Co 2/116th Regt

A Co 1/116th Regt

Rangers

(Above) The first assault wave was to hit fairly evenly along Omaha Beach, and then work inland through four exits. Heavy seas, the current and the heat of battle threw the landings off-kilter. (Insets, below and opposite) Famed combat photographer Robert Capa stumbled ashore with the 16th Infantry at the Easy Red/Fox Green section of Omaha Beach. Under fire, he snapped four rolls of "history in the making." Just eleven shots survived — including these three. (Opposite) Beach obstacles at Fox Green today, perhaps the very ones Capa snapped sheltering American soldiers.

Aiming for the Dune Line

A lot of responsibility rested on the young shoulders of twenty-three-year-old Joseph P. Vaghi, Jr. (inset, right). As Beachmaster, C-8 Platoon, 6th Naval Beach Battalion, he had the difficult task of controlling all traffic on the beach — both as personnel and equipment arrived and as the wounded and prisoners were evacuated. He still remembers his arrival on Omaha:

"The sound of screeching 12- and 14-inch shells from the warships USS Texas *and USS* Arkansas *offshore were sounds never heard by us before.... Rocket launchers mounted on landing craft moved in close to the shore and were spewing forth hundreds of rounds at a time onto the German defenses. Using the obstacles as shelter, we moved forward over the tidal flat under full enemy machine-gun fire until we finally reached the dune line. All C-8 made the long trek.... God was with us!"*

Two weeks later, Vaghi (below) was explaining the worth of invasion money to the villagers of St-Laurent-sur-Mer.

"I'd Wanted to Go to War"

Young Jack Hoffler of Hertford, North Carolina, (above) had a secret: when he had enlisted in August 1943, he was only fourteen. The recruiting officer in nearby Elizabeth City wasn't terribly particular: "As long as you could hold up your end of the stick," he'd gladly swear you in. Somehow Hoffler had made it through basic training undiscovered. Assigned as a gunner on what the navy called an LCVP (Landing Craft, Vehicle, Personnel), he was part of the first wave to hit Omaha Beach:

"When we came in — I don't know how to describe it — it was just a hell of a mess. There were explosions, guys lying dead on the beach, guys getting killed right there on the [landing craft's] ramp. I had to roll them off. I didn't know if they were alive or dead.... We must have been there twenty minutes. We loaded up with the wounded and then we went out again. Thirteen times we did that. Taking troops and supplies in and taking the wounded out.... I knew what I was doing. I knew what I had to do there. I'd wanted to go to war."

First Lieutenant Robert J. Rieske was an aide to Brigadier General Willard G. Wyman at the headquarters of the 1st Infantry Division. (Top) He photographed these American soldiers pinned down at Easy Red. In the distance at left stands one of the very few tanks that made it ashore. (Above) Rieske also scrawled this urgent message for Brigadier General Wyman, requesting reinforcements.

Although Ramsay bore full responsibility as naval c-in-c, he (like his British air colleagues) had to tread carefully in issuing direct orders to his American "subordinates" — since Britain was by now palpably the weaker and junior partner in the Atlantic alliance. The Americans' decision to start going ashore at 0630 was against his "advice," which was to go at 0700, just half an hour ahead of the British. The first wave thus began the run ashore in the dark as well as in a heavy swell. Rear Admiral J. L. Hall, USN, commanding Assault Force O, ignored some more British "advice" by choosing to launch his landing craft from as far out as twelve miles — to keep his ships out of range of enemy shore batteries. Allied intelligence had failed to appreciate that the German guns were positioned to enfilade the beaches rather than fire toward the sea (i.e., to shoot along the shore rather than over it, though capable of both). Launching from seven to two miles off, or even fewer, depending on local conditions, thus turned out to be a reasonable risk from which the British and Canadians generally profited.

The 741st Tank Battalion of twenty-nine Sherman DD tanks, capable of just four miles per hour in calm water, should have been launched from about two miles off Omaha so that the faster LCIs and LCAs would not reach the shore before them and be deprived of immediate armored support. But the tanks, with their curious inflatable canvas collars, were consigned to the swell early and twice as far out — and were thus unduly exposed to a strong crosswind, six-foot waves and the crosscurrent. Tragically, an order to launch much closer in because of the rough conditions did not reach the battalion. Twenty-seven

DD tanks broached and sank in one hundred feet of water about halfway out. Only two got ashore. (At Utah, none was lost; at Juno, the Canadian beach, only two sank.) The waves spilled over the collars, and seawater poured through the open hatches of the tank turrets. The LCT crews had apparently also made insufficient allowance for current, wind and waves and were swept seriously off course.

Among the first waves of troops going ashore at Omaha were men from Lieutenant Colonel James Earl Rudder's Ranger Force. The 2nd Battalion of the rangers, the U.S. Army's special forces (equivalent to the British commandos, with whom they had trained), had been given a fiendish task. They were to climb the cliffs at Pointe du Hoc, three miles west of the main landing beach, and capture the German heavy-gun battery on top — protected as it was by massive concrete casemates. The little promontory enabled the 155-mm guns to enfilade both Omaha and Utah Beaches. There was no tougher assignment on D-Day.

Half the battalion was to come ashore at the western extremity of the main landing, alongside the 116th Infantry, at 0630. One of three companies was then to march a mile or so southward with a detachment of the 116th Infantry and turn right to attack the battery in the rear. Two companies were held in reserve. Meanwhile, the other three companies — some 210 men — were to land directly beneath Pointe du Hoc and begin scaling it at 0730.

But like so much else at Omaha, the operation went badly wrong. The right-hand company of the 116th was all but annihilated on landing by massive German fire held back until the Americans were least able to assert themselves — as they came ashore. The rangers' C Company, having taken more than fifty percent casualties on leaving its British LCAs, was isolated at the western end of the main landing by a mile and a half of sand. Like so many other Americans on that nightmarish first day at Omaha, the survivors took shelter under the seawall or the bluff at the back of the beach.

A strong German defensive position, built around the break in the bluff at Vierville-sur-Mer — including trenches, bunkers and pillboxes, which the 116th had been unable to tackle — loomed almost directly above them. Nonetheless, the rangers climbed the bluff and attacked the defenses in the flank. A few men from the 116th managed to join them in a bitter engagement that lasted all day. Its main effect was to draw German fire that might otherwise have added to the carnage on the beach below.

More than ten thousand tons of high explosives from aircraft and the heaviest naval guns had been expended on the Pointe du Hoc battery before D-Day. Although the terrain on top of the cliff remains impressively cratered to this day, the concrete emplacements withstood the battering. Only the very rare direct hit made any real difference, and then not always.

The half-battalion of rangers ordered to make the frontal assault lost several landing craft on the way in, not to mention twenty men who were hauled back aboard ship after

(Opposite) The strain of those early hours at Omaha shows on the face of a medic at the foot of the cliffs that loomed a hundred feet above the beach. The 2nd Ranger Battalion had the unenviable task of scaling the cliffs at Pointe du Hoc (opposite, left inset). (Opposite, right inset) Members of the 2nd Rangers in action. (Below) The famous battalion's shoulder tab and diamond-shaped crest. (Bottom) Boots belonging to Sergeant Thomas J. Ruggiero, a ranger who was shot through the side as he left his landing craft but nevertheless made it to the top of the cliffs.

falling into the sea with their heavy kit while trying to transfer to their landing craft. Other craft drifted eastward on the current and had to turn to run westward along the shoreline — making the assault party half an hour late. The Germans directed an increasing volume of fire at the Americans. Two Allied destroyers came in close to give covering fire, providing some relief for the rangers as the incoming tide swallowed up the beach below the cliffs.

Despite having lost much of their climbing equipment, the rangers fired rockets attached to ropes and grapnels up the cliff. Only a few caught in the heavy soil — but they were enough to enable nearly two hundred men to scramble to the top, despite many casualties from machine guns and showers of grenades. The pre-arranged signal "Praise the Lord" informed the American higher command just after 0730 that the rangers had surmounted the cliffs. The tide had already reduced their little beach to almost nothing. Colonel Rudder, who set up his headquarters in a captured German bunker, was confident enough to signal his reserve and the other ranger battalion on hand — the 5th — to land to the east with the regular infantry. The men from the 2nd Battalion's D, E and F Companies got on with the grim business of driving the enemy out of his trenches and pillboxes — and out of the gun emplacements themselves.

Which were devoid of guns. They had been moved inland after the preliminary bombing began and replaced in the casemates by five wooden telegraph poles. Remarkably, the survivors of the climb and the fierce gun battles in and around the German redoubt at the top suppressed their disappointment and carried on clearing the German defenses in close-quarters fighting. Some four dozen rangers followed deep wheel tracks inland and found the five guns — undamaged, and unmanned. Complete with mounds of ammunition, they were neatly lined up in the open about a thousand yards back from the cliff edge. In their new position they were still a threat to Utah Beach, less than eight miles to the west, and could also have fired at the invasion fleet. By 0900 on D-Day, the Americans had disabled the guns with grenades and also blown up a large ammunition dump set well back from the guns. Despite seventy-five percent casualties, the rangers beat off all counterattacks and hung on to Pointe du Hoc. It was a truly heroic feat — the first American victory in Normandy.

DOWN BELOW ON OMAHA BEACH, CATASTROPHE THREATENED. TWO HOURS AFTER STARTING to land at 0630, the 1st Division had some five thousand men ashore out of the fifty-five thousand in V Corps. They had come nowhere near clearing the exits through the breaks in the bluff — which was meant to be done in the first hour. They had little equipment beyond small arms. A glut of wrecked and broken-down vehicles cluttered the

By 0730, the cliffs at Pointe du Hoc were secure (opposite, left inset) and reinforcements from the 5th Ranger Battalion began coming ashore (opposite, right inset). (Opposite) The cliffs today.

Heading out from Omaha

Nineteen-year-old Thomas E. Herring (below) of C Company, 5th Ranger Battalion, was lucky to make it ashore at Omaha Beach. He had jumped from his LCA into water over his head and nearly drowned — with 90 pounds of gear strapped to his 135-pound body:

"The carnage on the beach was indescribable.... Although many wounded were crying for help, aid-men were scarce and others could not help because they had an assigned task to accomplish. After a few minutes of protection from the seawall, some rangers blew gaps in the defensive barbed wire with torpedoes and we vaulted the seawall and set about climbing the steep hill to our objective — a road paralleling the beach and leading to Pointe du Hoc. When we reached the road atop the hill, we were greeted with heavy machine-gun fire from German gun emplacements farther inland. We set up to eliminate the enemy gun positions.... When our mortar shells began to land, in their traversing fire pattern, one could see bodies, guns and dirt flying everywhere."

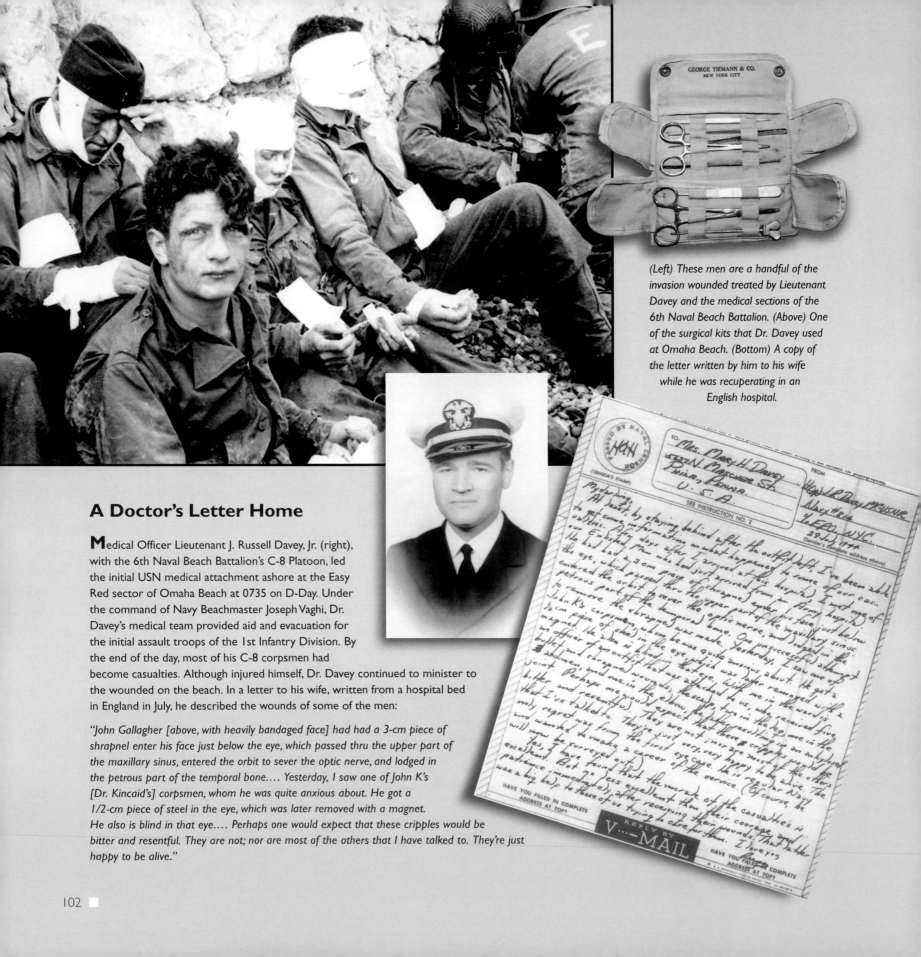

(Left) These men are a handful of the invasion wounded treated by Lieutenant Davey and the medical sections of the 6th Naval Beach Battalion. (Above) One of the surgical kits that Dr. Davey used at Omaha Beach. (Bottom) A copy of the letter written by him to his wife while he was recuperating in an English hospital.

A Doctor's Letter Home

Medical Officer Lieutenant J. Russell Davey, Jr. (right), with the 6th Naval Beach Battalion's C-8 Platoon, led the initial USN medical attachment ashore at the Easy Red sector of Omaha Beach at 0735 on D-Day. Under the command of Navy Beachmaster Joseph Vaghi, Dr. Davey's medical team provided aid and evacuation for the initial assault troops of the 1st Infantry Division. By the end of the day, most of his C-8 corpsmen had become casualties. Although injured himself, Dr. Davey continued to minister to the wounded on the beach. In a letter to his wife, written from a hospital bed in England in July, he described the wounds of some of the men:

"John Gallagher [above, with heavily bandaged face] had had a 3-cm piece of shrapnel enter his face just below the eye, which passed thru the upper part of the maxillary sinus, entered the orbit to sever the optic nerve, and lodged in the petrous part of the temporal bone.... Yesterday, I saw one of John K's [Dr. Kincaid's] corpsmen, whom he was quite anxious about. He got a 1/2-cm piece of steel in the eye, which was later removed with a magnet. He also is blind in that eye.... Perhaps one would expect that these cripples would be bitter and resentful. They are not; nor are most of the others that I have talked to. They're just happy to be alive."

(Above) Artist Dwight Shepler, aboard the destroyer USS *Emmons*, chronicled the drama in the waters off Omaha Beach as American destroyers pounded German battery positions. (Below) Members of the 16th Infantry Regiment rest and tend to injuries on a narrow strip of shingle before undertaking the assault on the cliff above.

shallows and the beach that was steadily shrinking as the tide came in. At 0830, landings were called off for lack of space. General Bradley aboard the cruiser USS *Augusta* gave serious thought to abandoning the beach and shifting the rest of V Corps to Utah and/or eastward to the British Gold Beach. Like his subordinates afloat and ashore, he was caught in the fog of war — a clear overview was physically impossible in the smoke, and the situation looked even worse than it was.

The eleven destroyers of Bombardment Force C came as close inshore as they could and, with the few operable tanks on the beach, pounded German bunkers and pillboxes. The only way off, given that the Germans still controlled the exits, was through the barbed wire, up and over the seawall and the bluff behind it. Gradually — and, it seemed, spontaneously (there were hardly any radios) — small groups of soldiers from the 16th and 116th Regiments and the 5th Rangers began to scramble up to the top of the ridge at various points between the heavily blocked exits. One or two larger armed landing craft forced their way through the chaos at the water's edge, firing on German strongpoints as they came. More troops and tanks piled ashore to the east of the clutter at Vierville-sur-Mer, creating more chaos as various units landed in the wrong places.

But by lunchtime Bradley was sufficiently encouraged by the first penetrations inland to recommit to Omaha. The groups of American soldiers who had made it to the top began to join up and make attacks on the German coastal defenses from behind. The enemy's static defense units, such as the local 709th Division, seemed to be truly

Bringing the Troops Ashore

Although nineteen-year-old Howard B. Clarkson (left) and the other crewmembers of *LCI-537* considered themselves "rookies," they did their best to land members of the 1st Infantry Division at Omaha Beach as close to shore as possible. The beach (above), studded with obstacles and mines, was raked by deadly German fire throughout the day:

"My beaching station was as an operator of the stern anchor winch.... As we headed in, I said a silent prayer: 'Please, Lord, let me do this right this time.' More than once in training I failed to get a proper purchase on the bottom with the anchor, with the result that another LCI had to help us off the beach.... Later that night we anchored among the hundreds of other ships and listened to the sound of gunfire inland.... We paused in a silent prayer for all those 'Willies and Joes' from the 1st Infantry that we had put ashore that day."

static — failing to withdraw before being cut off piecemeal, killed in their bunkers or surrendering. Many of these troops were pressed men from conquered Eastern Europe; many taken prisoner could not speak German, let alone English. And the Germans began to run out of ammunition, especially for their deadly artillery. But their snipers continued to take a steady toll.

As the Americans began to move inland from the top of the bluff, elements of the 352nd Infantry Division (a more formidable unit whose presence had not been registered by Allied intelligence) did fall back — on another advantageous defensive feature. The terrain behind the coast was commonly made up of small fields surrounded by thick hedges with sunken roads running between them. This Normandy *bocage*, or hedgerow country — of which very little survived the century — would soon become a curse on the Allied campaign. The hedges were not merely ideal for snipers or machine-gunners; they could also comfortably conceal columns of tanks.

By lunchtime the Americans had taken undefended Vierville-sur-Mer, the village overlooking one of the exits from Omaha earmarked for vehicles — but pockets of U.S. troops nearby were still surrounded by Germans. Yet vehicles and men could now use the exit and advance inland from there. The house-to-house battle with men of the 352nd for the next village east — St-Laurent-sur-Mer — ended in stalemate as night fell.

Colleville-sur-Mer, next in line eastward, came under such heavy fire from the warships firing almost blind into the smoky haze that scores of American troops were killed by friendly fire. The radio sets that might have saved them littered the seabed off Omaha. A standoff occurred there too as darkness descended. By that time, the corps and

(Left) A helmet bearing the distinctive blue and gray symbol of the 29th Infantry Division, which provided the 116th Infantry to the first wave at Omaha early on the morning of June 6. The 116th, a National Guard unit from Virginia, suffered terrible losses — including nineteen young men from the small town of Bedford.

Surviving Bloody Omaha

Separated on arrival at Omaha from members of the 5th Engineers Special Brigade and C-9 Platoon of the 6th Naval Beach Battalion, Seaman 1st Class Robert Giguere quickly made himself useful wherever he could. After helping blow up a major gun emplacement, he rescued five members of the French Underground [Resistance] from a church basement in Colleville-sur-Mer just before it was blown up by naval bombardment:

"I told the officer I was a navy man and had to get back to the beach to do my job. So myself, the five French Underground people, and some of the army walking wounded went back to the beach. I was still looking for my outfit going up the beach when I was blown up by mortar or artillery. I must have been knocked unconscious because when I came to, I was in the 40th Army Hospital in Cirencester, England. It was June 10 — my eighteenth birthday."

Hospital at Sea

Joe B. Williams (below), a carpenter's mate third class on the USS *Bayfield*, helped deal with the wounded just off Utah Beach in the first days after D-Day:

"LCIs (above) were delivering casualties to the Bayfield on a constant basis. The ship was being used as an auxiliary hospital ship until the wounded men could be picked up and taken back to England. There were wounded everywhere — in sick bay, in the mess hall and in the passageways — [and] you couldn't walk anywhere. We saw German prisoners of war in crafts alongside our ship although they weren't being taken on board. Some looked so young, maybe fourteen to sixteen years old; others looked like they were seventy. Their faces were so sad."

divisional staffs had come ashore and sixty percent of their men had managed to land. More than twenty thousand men in a second wave were ready to reinforce them from daybreak on June 7.

The Germans were not defeated — far from it — but they had failed to throw the invaders back into the sea as intended. And they were tired, broken up into often ad hoc groups that had been committed piecemeal to the fighting. The Americans, having got a foothold, albeit much smaller than planned for Day One, were already in the happy position of being able to reinforce and resupply faster than the defenders could from inland — the calculation on which the entire Normandy enterprise was based. Inland, Allied aircraft shot up any enemy unit on the move by day, as Lieutenant Colonel Fritz Ziegelmann of the 352nd Division staff recalled:

At about 1100 hours the weather conditions changed. The sun broke through the clouds and it was now high tide. The first enemy fighter-bombers appeared before long and started to paste the very widely spaced marching groups of the reinforced 915th Infantry Regiment [of the 352nd Division]. The movements ceased since more and more fighter-bombers appeared. By this continuous movement of fighter-bombers at the coast almost every movement on our side was made impossible.... A request to the supply group of the 352nd produced the information that we should not count on a fresh ammunition delivery for three more days.

(Opposite, right) With arms raised in surrender, German prisoners of war at Omaha Beach are marched down toward the shore. (Below) A makeshift grave at Omaha Beach.

THE CASUALTIES WERE HIGHER ON OMAHA THAN ANYWHERE ELSE IN THE INVASION ZONE. Some 2,400 Americans were killed, wounded or captured from the 1st and 29th Divisions, compared with about half that from the 352nd — but the German division had lost twenty percent of its total strength, compared with the Americans' seven. It was all but a broken division by nightfall on D-Day. The weight of numbers and the cornucopian quantities of equipment, munitions and supplies had done it for the Americans. The other factor was the sheer persistent courage of their men against the initial advantages of the well-entrenched defenders who prevented the U.S. Army from achieving nearly all of its objectives for D-Day.

"On the port side aft, dead soldiers were stacked up like cardboard. Helmets were in a big pile."
— Robert E. Adams, U.S. Coast Guard, picking up the dead at Omaha Beach

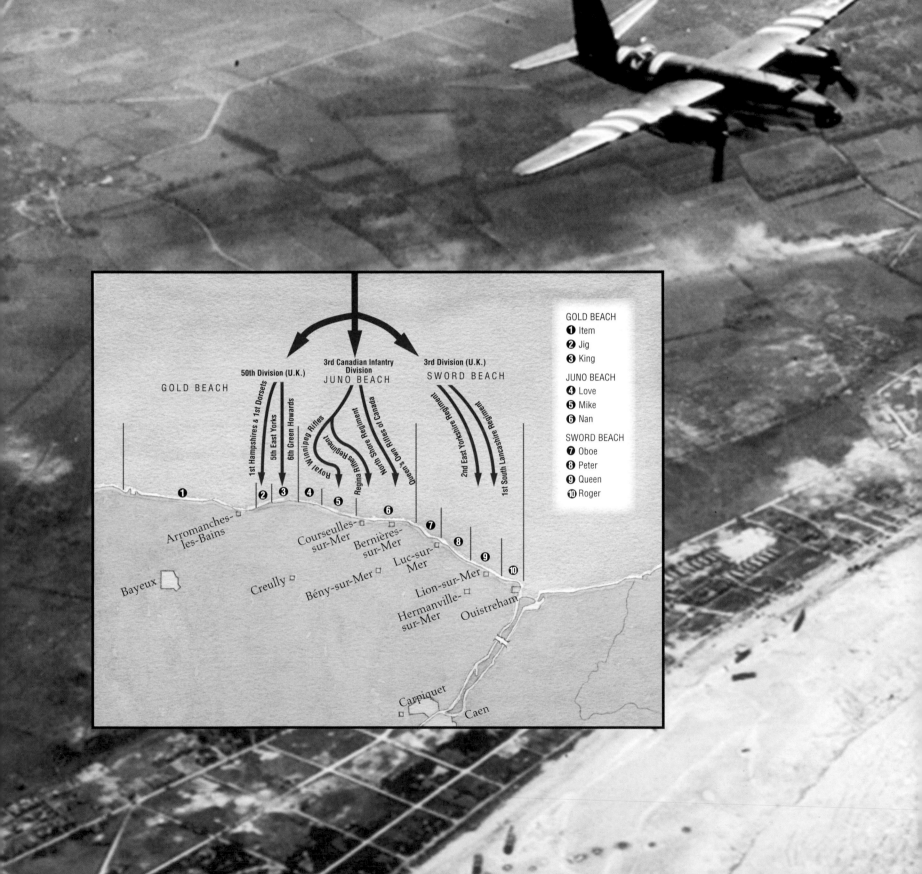

GOLD BEACH

50th Division (U.K.)

3rd Canadian Infantry Division
JUNO BEACH

3rd Division (U.K.)
SWORD BEACH

1st Hampshires & 1st Dorsets

5th East Yorks

6th Green Howards

Royal Winnipeg Rifles

Regina Rifles Regiment

North Shore Regiment

Queen's Own Rifles of Canada

2nd East Yorkshire Regiment

1st South Lancashire Regiment

GOLD BEACH
❶ Item
❷ Jig
❸ King

JUNO BEACH
❹ Love
❺ Mike
❻ Nan

SWORD BEACH
❼ Oboe
❽ Peter
❾ Queen
❿ Roger

Arromanches-les-Bains

Courseulles-sur-Mer

Bernières-sur-Mer

Luc-sur-Mer

Lion-sur-Mer

Hermanville-sur-Mer

Ouistreham

Bayeux

Creully

Bény-sur-Mer

Carpiquet

Caen

Sword, Juno and Gold

**"My hands grew numb and dead and my
teeth were chattering with cold and fright."**

— Captain J. H. Patterson, a medical officer
with 4 Commando, en route to Sword Beach

■ THE LANDINGS ON THE EASTERN SEGMENT of the invasion front were made by the British 2nd Army, under Lieutenant General Sir Miles Dempsey — and its men were delivered by the Eastern Task Force, under Rear Admiral Philip Vian. The assault force was led ashore on each beach by DD tanks (though some arrived late) and consisted of three infantry divisions: the 3rd British, which landed at Sword Beach; the 3rd Canadian at Juno (the Canadians would soon build up to a corps and finally to a whole army); and the 50th British at Gold. Self-propelled artillery and armored units followed close on the heels of the infantry.

The three beaches remain perfect for leisure purposes, weather permitting. They are similar in appearance to the American beaches (though Omaha is steeper) — broad, evenly sloping, hard, golden sand, backed by soft sand and then dunes (the shingle has by now all but disappeared), with a coastal road running behind that links a series of small fishing villages a few miles apart. Roadways leading from the beach to these settlements were earmarked as exits. The villages have in many cases grown since the war, but the gaps between them still widen from east to west. There is no forbidding, Omaha-style bluff immediately behind any of the chosen beaches, but higher ground begins a mile or two inland of Gold and Juno (where there was a high seawall at Bernières-sur-Mer).

There is very little left of the bocage — the dense pattern of small fields surrounded by immense hedgerows with sunken roads between them — that would prove so difficult for the troops advancing inland, and such a boon for the defenders. The terrain inland from Sword, immediately to the west of the mouth of the river Orne and its port of Ouistreham, is generally flat with few trees. In 1944 it was marshy in places, if not defensively flooded by the Germans.

AMONG THE FIRST TO GO ASHORE AT THE EASTERN END OF SWORD — THE EASTERNMOST OF THE five beaches — were Lord Lovat's 1st Special Service Brigade. Leading the main seaborne assault on Sword Beach was the 8th Infantry Brigade Group, preceded by a regiment of DD tanks (13th/18th Hussars) and to be followed at two-hour intervals by the other two brigades of the 3rd Infantry Division (Major General T. G. Rennie). Behind them was the rest of I British Corps (Lieutenant General J. T. Crocker), part of the 2nd Army.

Ramsay Bader of the 511th Battery, 147th Field Regiment, Royal Artillery, was the driver of a self-propelled gun, a heavy 25-pounder cannon on a tank hull:

> We fired as we went in, and also as we were being shelled by the German heavy guns…. It wasn't all that easy with the mortars, the shells that were coming over, a lot of casualties…even with our rocket ships alongside and [a battleship] firing salvos…. The first tank off the LCT somehow didn't make it. I was the next off…. We seemed to make it, whether it was luck or what: we kept going and we made the shore with our guns firing and a lot of other tanks.

"Get off the beach — off the beach, off the bloody beach, get forward lads and give the buggers hell!"

— A Green Howards platoon commander

It was even worse for the infantry, as Private Peter Brown of the 4th Platoon, C Company, 2nd Battalion, East Yorkshire Regiment, attested. He found the cross-channel passage on the LSI "cramped, boring and tense." Sent ashore in the second wave of the first assault, shortly after H-Hour, he was shocked to see the upended bow of a new Norwegian destroyer, the *Svenner*, that had been sunk by a German mine:

> *Apart from that, I was so terribly seasick that nothing else registered, really. All I wanted to do was to get ashore and get out of the landing craft. I remember the doors going down and charging [over them]. We landed in about three feet of water and waded ashore.... [There were] quite a few bodies floating about from A and B Companies [in the first wave]. There was a tank, I remember, knocked out, and we took shelter behind that.*

MONTGOMERY'S PRIMARY OBJECTIVE FOR DAY ONE OF THE INVASION WAS CAEN, CAPITAL OF Normandy and the key to German regional communications and command. It was his most important target. Only slightly less important was the high ground east and southeast of the city, needed for fighter airfields. Sword Beach was wide enough for a simultaneous landing by two brigades, with a third in close support. But the 3rd Division's three brigades landed one at a time at what still seem remarkably relaxed intervals of two hours. The 8th Brigade's task was to clear the beach, and the 185th Brigade was to spearhead the attack on Caen. The 9th Brigade was also headed for that city.

The German 716th Division, led by Lieutenant General Wilhelm Richter, was the static, coastal-defense formation whose area included Sword, Juno and part of Gold beaches —

(Top) A medic attends to wounded men in the shelter of an AVRE Petard belonging to the 79th Assault Squadron, Royal Engineers, on the Queen Red sector of Sword Beach. To the right stands an M-10 antitank gun. (Above) A number of Lord Lovat's commandos, sporting berets, crouch in the foreground before heading inland.

Moving the Men Inland

The Royal Navy commandos came in with the first wave to direct subsequent landings and to help soldiers move inland. Ken Oakley (left) of Fox Commando was assigned to protect and assist Beachmaster Lieutenant John Church on Sword Beach at all times — even if it meant ignoring the cries of wounded men:

"We were quickly out of the landing craft and running up the sandy beach as mortar and machine-gun fire sped us on our way. At the high-water mark, we went to ground to take stock of the situation and get our bearings. John said we had landed almost exactly in our scheduled area...but the mortar fire became more intense. More and more landing craft were beaching and we were kept busy persuading army personnel not to stay on the beach to brew their tea but to go and chase those Germans who were still shelling us. The flail tanks and other 'Funnies' had done a good job in clearing mines from the beach and we were getting good exit lanes marked down leading to a road."

(Below, top) Men from Lord Lovat's brigade leave the beach around 1000 hours, slowing down to single-file formation as they thread their way along a narrow path across a minefield. By this time, regular infantry had neutralized most of the German opposition. (Middle) Using a tank for cover, infantrymen deal with an isolated sniper. (Bottom) Commandos in the nearby town of Ouistreham scramble behind Sherman DD tanks as they come under harassing fire.

the rest of which, along with the American beaches, was covered by the stronger 352nd Infantry Division. But the 2nd Army was unaware of the presence of the 21st Panzer Division on and near the coast — especially its two grenadier regiments on either side of the Orne estuary. (It was thought to be much farther inland.)

This division, commanded by Major General Edgar Feuchtinger, had been deployed forward, albeit piecemeal, by Rommel — and was thus the only fully mobile German army division in a position to interfere with events on the eastern flank of the Allied invasion at its very beginning. It had served under Rommel in his brilliant North African campaign but was all but destroyed in May 1943 and had been re-formed with drafts and tanks of frequently indifferent quality. Yet it would play a disproportionate and often gallant role in resisting the first landings in the Caen area. Its elderly or captured French tanks were initially stationed south of Caen, its artillery on the heights south of the city and its two panzer-grenadier (armored infantry) regiments on either side of the river Orne — the boundary between the 7th Army in Normandy and the 15th to its east, guarding the Pas de Calais. It was thus divided between the two armies, and the divisional history noted:

For a formation like a panzer division, which can only achieve its full effect in a unified attack, things could hardly be worse.

The division also was not immune from the uncertainty that would seriously affect German resistance for some two weeks:

Anxiety about further landings at some other place along the lengthy coast from Le Havre to Calais remained, and became one of the most fateful elements of the entire battle for Normandy.

THE OVERCAUTIOUS LANDING ON A ONE-BRIGADE FRONT WAS NO WAY TO CAPTURE A PLACE like Caen, which was certain to be strongly defended. The plan looks unrealistic, and not only in hindsight. And while the 2nd Army's orders to the 3rd British Division to take it on D-Day were unequivocal, the I British Corps hedged its bets by ordering the division, "should the enemy forestall us at Caen," to refrain from further assaults and "contain the enemy" there. In the end it was a British pulled punch.

The lead brigade — the 8th — advanced three miles inland to the Periers Ridge, where the British had to fight hard to overcome a German coastal command post and a nearby strongpoint. It took them until lunchtime. The 185th Brigade started out for Caen but farther along the same ridge ran into elements of the 192nd Panzer-Grenadier Regiment. One of three battalions (the 2nd Shropshires) got to within three miles of the center of the city and one mile short of its northern suburbs but was halted by German tanks concealed in a wood. It would be five weeks —not five hours — before Caen finally fell to the Canadians.

An independent tank brigade was supposed to follow the 3rd Division inland but it got bogged down on the chaotic beach. Events on all beaches showed that the high

The Drive for Caen

G. C. A. Gilbert (below), later a major general, was a captain with C Company, 2nd Battalion, the Royal Lincolnshire Regiment, which landed at Sword Beach:

"The big...question [facing] the 3rd Division...was whether we should have got to Caen.... The bombing of the Brigade Headquarters...certainly held it all up because it had to be reconstituted and the battalion had to be re-coordinated.... So we got I suppose about three, four miles down. I should think that we were probably level with Pegasus Bridge.... By then [the Germans] had reinforced very rapidly and there were two German top-quality divisions around Caen within a matter of a few days.... We got into an eyeball-to-eyeball confrontation.... It's interesting looking back on it, whether or not, if we had captured [Caen], we would have, quite frankly, managed to hold it. I like to think we would have done, but.... "

(Above left) A Royal Marines Centaur tank, with its distinctive calibrated turret. (Above right) A tank belonging to the Royal Marines Armoured Support Group moves through the village of Langrune-sur-Mer, not far from the dividing line between Juno and Sword Beaches. (Below) A Royal Marines Centaur on display today not far from Pegasus Bridge.

command had underestimated the complexity of landing large armored forces — especially with major infantry units in the area. Hardly any British tanks were able to break out of the traffic jam on the sands to support the drive for Caen. When the 9th Brigade, the divisional reserve, was diverted eastward at lunchtime to support the paratroops and commandos in defense of the captured Orne and canal bridges, the front line congealed — and any hope of a quick capture of Caen was lost.

The unexpected presence of German tanks and the absence of British ones enabled the 21st Panzers to foil Montgomery's attempt to capture Caen on D-Day and to stall his entire campaign — quite a feat for a scattered and understrength division. Meanwhile, the more dangerous 12th SS Panzer Division was coming up from inland Lisieux.

(Inset) A sergeant from 5 Beach Group (in foreground at right) directs traffic as British troops and tanks advance through the village of Hermanville-sur-Mer, about a mile inland from Sword Beach. (Above) The same location in the village today.

"We were so intent on getting to the beach that if the engines had stopped or broken down, sheer willpower alone would have driven the craft ashore."

— Captain Jack Fawcett, 1st Battalion, Canadian Scottish Regiment, heading for Juno Beach

LESS THAN THREE MILES WEST OF SWORD WAS JUNO BEACH — ASSIGNED TO FIFTEEN THOUSAND Canadian troops, supported by some nine thousand British. Like the Americans and the British, the Canadians relied on their own bombers and warships — including minesweepers and bombardment vessels — to support their country's troops. Some 230 RCAF bombers working with the RAF dropped 850 tons of bombs on coastal batteries on the eve of D-Day. As elsewhere, direct hits in the poor weather were few and far between. The coastal batteries in the Juno area were medium at best, in some places incomplete, and made no significant contribution to German resistance.

As with the other assault beaches, enemy naval and air forces failed to intervene. Only their previously laid mines troubled the Canadians, and considerably at that. However, there appears to be no record of any German gun battery hitting any Allied ship on D-Day — one of several inexplicable facts about the invasion.

After the heavy air and naval bombardments, the very last of the preparatory attacks on the assault area was a program of "beach-drenching fire" by lighter naval guns. Two Canadian ships were among the eleven destroyers that swept Juno with shellfire just before the landing. Smaller gunboats worked closer in, peppering enemy defenses even as the landing craft started to come ashore. This lighter bombardment could not destroy the heavier concrete structures but did force the Germans to take cover, even at the four main coastal strongpoints facing the Canadians.

As self-propelled guns and tanks approached the shore, they joined in the drenching — often blasting away even before they left their landing craft, firing over the heads of the infantrymen in their LCAs. The drenching went on for about half an hour and included mass launches of rockets in the last minutes before H-Hour. The effect of all this was mainly psychological, unnerving some defenders and cheering the approaching invaders. Postwar studies revealed that perhaps one German defensive structure in seven was knocked out, but huge damage was done to the fabric of seaside villages. There was much overshooting, perhaps out of consideration for the infantry, but no reliable means of measuring the real effect. However, it was noted that German resistance was stiffer from strongpoints that had not been subjected to it.

(Opposite) A Royal Canadian Navy landing craft heads toward Juno Beach. (Above) Members of the Royal Winnipeg Rifles en route to the Mike Red and Mike Green sectors of Juno as part of the first assault wave.

When Duty Calls

Corporal Gerald Pawson (below) was to be best man at his sister's wedding in Leeds, England, on June 6. But as a member of the Royal Canadian Electrical and Mechanical Engineers (RCEME) serving with the 3rd Canadian Infantry Division, he was locked up with the invasion force from June 2 and could not notify his family. Planes flying overhead on their way to Normandy on the morning of June 6 delivered the message instead. Once Pawson's family realized he would not be at the wedding, they began the ceremony with a prayer for all of the soldiers, sailors and airmen taking part in the invasion. Pawson still vividly remembers that morning:

"The sea was so rough and we were so seasick, it really didn't matter what was waiting for us as long as we were getting off that bloody bouncing boat.... Later I remember thinking that I would much rather have been at my little sister's wedding than in a hole a couple of miles inside France still suffering from the sea trip."

117

A Life Preserver with My Name on It

The LCT carrying Canadian soldier Stanley "Fish" Seneco (below) of A Squadron, 1st Hussars, hit a mine while approaching Juno Beach and he was forced to abandon his tank:

"The waves took the dinghy so fast that I ended up swimming for my life. I took my pistol out of my holster and put it in my jacket — why, I don't know. I was a few yards away from the tank and having a tough time staying afloat and was just ready to give up when my ATEA (life preserver) came floating out of the tank. It had "Fish" written all over it and I grabbed it. A team of horses couldn't have pulled it away from me. Then, after what seemed like a very long time, Johnny Pearson came out in another dinghy from another LCT that had been blown up and pulled me in. When the tide went out in the afternoon, we were able to walk ashore."

The assault formation for Juno was the 3rd Canadian Division (Major General R. F. L. Keller), under command of the 2nd Army. A main objective was the airfield at Carpiquet, east of Caen, and the surrounding area. The 1st Hussars and the Fort Garry Horse armored regiments landed first with their tanks — closely followed by the 7th and 8th Infantry Brigades, with the 9th standing by at sea in reserve. The LSIs arrived offshore at the right time and in the right positions, launching their loaded landing craft from the davits normally used for lifeboats. But the landing-craft formations were soon disrupted by the poor sea conditions, and a total of ninety were lost to the sea, collisions, mines or enemy action off Juno — a slightly higher loss rate than on the two British beaches. As well, landing holdups denied the demolition squads most of the time they needed to destroy beach obstacles. (They had to wait to deal with them at the next low tide in the evening.) Much damage was therefore done to LCAs returning to their motherships for more troops.

At first, the heaviest weapons used against them were mortars (which were bad enough), supported by medium and light machine guns. The landing craft were less than two miles off Juno before the enemy opened erratic and desultory fire. This intensified, however, once the troops were ashore.

Some infantry got ashore ahead of their tanks as the heavy sea disrupted carefully calculated landing schedules. The right, or western, flank of the Canadian landing was assigned to the 7th Brigade, where the tanks managed to arrive up to twenty minutes ahead of the infantry. Many of those that arrived late settled in shallow water and opened fire over

(Right) The first wave of Canadian forces landing at Juno Beach were equipped with a modified version of the traditional British helmet — sometimes referred to as an "invasion" helmet. Beside it is the highly classified plan carried by every Allied unit, detailing its place of landing and specific mission.

(Inset) This now-famous still from the 1945 British documentary *The True Glory* shows Canadian troops going ashore at the Nan Red sector of Juno Beach. The larger photograph is of the same location today — although the house that dominated the view from the landing craft on June 6, 1944, now boasts an addition in front.

the German beach obstacles. The rough weather forced the navy to bring the tank-landing ships right up to the beach instead of launching the DD tanks from well offshore, despite a plethora of uncleared mines. Some tanks sank in the five-foot waves but most of them rumbled and squeaked up the firm sand safely, enabling the troopers of the 1st Hussars and the Fort Garry Horse to give covering fire.

The sea conditions delayed the arrival of the Queen's Own Rifles of Canada (a Toronto regiment in the 8th Brigade) by nearly half an hour after a rough passage from seven miles out. These first Canadian soldiers shook off their seasickness and waded onto an even more menacing terra firma at 0812 — facing a 200-yard dash across the beach and fire from an undamaged and unspotted "resistance nest" complete with 88-mm antitank gun. Their first objective was the village of Bernières-sur-Mer. On their left (to the east) the North Shore Regiment from New Brunswick was assigned Saint-Aubin, while the Régiment de la Chaudière waited in reserve.

To the right of the 8th Brigade, the 7th assigned the right flank of the assault to the Regina Rifles, who were ordered to attack the unscathed strongpoint covering Courseulles-sur-Mer and then the village itself. The Royal Winnipeg Rifles landed to their left as a company of the 1st Battalion, the Canadian Scottish Regiment, was held in reserve. The 9th Brigade (the Highland Light Infantry of Canada; the Stormont, Dundas and Glengarry Highlanders; and the North Nova Scotia Highlanders), backed by the tanks of the Sherbrooke Fusiliers, was the divisional reserve, which landed about two and a half hours later.

Juno Beach was not as smooth as Sword, and the planned breakout of the 9th Brigade was held up by another huge jam of vehicles. Each Canadian brigade experienced serious delays before the narrow exits could be cleared by a combination of artillery bombardment, bulldozers and heavy explosions set off by engineers. The defense was not as stiff as at Omaha but much damage was still

"There were about thirty men in our landing craft. Eight…were killed; two of us were wounded."

— Rolph Jackson, Queen's Own Rifles of Canada

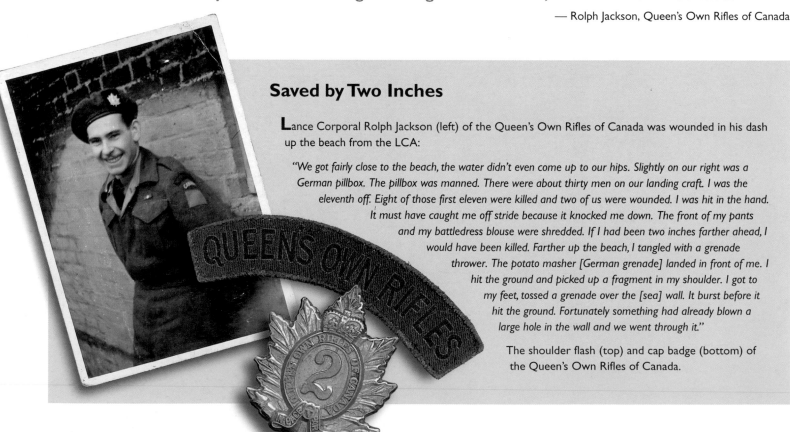

Saved by Two Inches

Lance Corporal Rolph Jackson (left) of the Queen's Own Rifles of Canada was wounded in his dash up the beach from the LCA:

"We got fairly close to the beach, the water didn't even come up to our hips. Slightly on our right was a German pillbox. The pillbox was manned. There were about thirty men on our landing craft. I was the eleventh off. Eight of those first eleven were killed and two of us were wounded. I was hit in the hand. It must have caught me off stride because it knocked me down. The front of my pants and my battledress blouse were shredded. If I had been two inches farther ahead, I would have been killed. Farther up the beach, I tangled with a grenade thrower. The potato masher [German grenade] landed in front of me. I hit the ground and picked up a fragment in my shoulder. I got to my feet, tossed a grenade over the [sea] wall. It burst before it hit the ground. Fortunately something had already blown a large hole in the wall and we went through it."

The shoulder flash (top) and cap badge (bottom) of the Queen's Own Rifles of Canada.

(Above and below) These rare images of Canadian troops arriving at Juno Beach were taken by Telegrapher James Grant of the Royal Canadian Navy, who served aboard one of the landing craft. (Inset) This house, which still dominates the beach at Bernières-sur-Mer, is believed to be the first residence liberated along the Normandy beaches on June 6.

Flying Reconnaissance over Normandy

Flight Lieutenant James B. Prendergast (below, with his aircraft) and the other members of the Royal Canadian Air Force, 430 Squadron, 39 Reconnaissance Wing, flew low-level reconnaissance missions as the "eyes of the 2nd British Army." Prendergast flew three sorties in his Mustang I *Lazy Lady* over the Normandy beachhead on D-Day. Toward the end of his first sortie, as he headed to the east and south of Caen, he spotted a number of tanks entering the woods in the Villers-Bocage area. "This, I realized, was a panzer division that I had not been briefed to look for. Quite a surprise!" Upon returning to base and reporting his find, Prendergast was sent back to verify the size of the force:

"I saw activity spread over a wide area and satisfied myself that there was a substantial division down there…. Later I was informed that the presence of this panzer division was not expected."

(Opposite) A Mustang, sporting black and white invasion stripes, flies reconnaissance over Normandy in a painting by Flight Lieutenant Eric Aldwinckle.

Landing craft were not the only victims of the obstacles scattered in the waters and along the invasion beaches. (Above) This Bren carrier, the workhorse tracked vehicle used by the British and Canadian armies, hit a landmine before it could even reach shore.

done by enemy machine guns and snipers.

M. Jean Houel, a French civilian living in the village of Courseulles-sur-Mer just behind the beach, was overjoyed to see the khaki tide coming up the sand — even though his brother had been wounded in the bombardment:

> *I remember it as if it were today. The Canadians who landed [were] from the Régiment de la Chaudière. At 7 A.M., there they were…. When I went out, suddenly I saw a tall fellow in front of me with a typically English helmet, and I said [in English]: "Here they are, the Tommies!" and the young man answered in French: "Je suis Canadien" [I am a Canadian].*

LANCE CORPORAL EDWARD KENDALL WAS AN ORDERLY IN THE 46TH FIELD SURGICAL Unit of the Royal Army Medical Corps, attached to the Canadian 3rd Division. He was one of an eleven-strong team of very mixed origins — typical of the armies of civilians in uniform pouring onto the beaches. They took their mobile operating theater across the Channel in an uncomfortable LST, where they had to sleep on stretchers beneath their vehicles. On arrival off Juno they transferred to a "Rhino" — a vast raft assembled from barges, capable of carrying up

(Above) This concrete emplacement behind the seawall at the village of Bernières-sur-Mer originally held a 50-mm antitank gun. (Inset, left) Wounded Canadian soldiers from the first assault waves lie in the shelter of the seawall as they wait to be evacuated. (Inset, right) Later on June 6, German POWs were gathered here before being shipped off to England.

to forty vehicles and powered by two huge outboard motors — for the last quarter-mile to the beach. Reassured by the firm sand, they drove along the beach in their truck to a position where they could "set up shop," until:

> *Suddenly the motor stalled. There we were, a sitting target with a three-ton lorry and couldn't start the motor. Our driver…Mac…was swearing like a trooper. Major [J. M.] Leggett, cool as a cucumber, said, "We'll have to push…. Get behind the truck," and we got it going and we all jumped on…. We had been operating when a lot of fireworks were going on outside…. We ducked more or less under the operating table. [Leggett would] just turn round and say, "Gentlemen, shall we carry on?"*

The fight for Courseulles was a hard one. Two companies of the Winnipegs, known as the "Little Black Devils," were decimated to the west of the town by more Germans who had escaped the preliminary bombardments. Some Chaudières joined this fight after being forced to swim ashore (all but one of A Company's LCAs foundered). In all, 340 Canadians died, 574 were wounded and 47 captured in the assault. (The Allied command had feared casualties twice as high.) The only Canadian unit to reach its D-Day objective was the 1st Hussars, west of Caen — a rare feat among those involved in the first wave.

D-Day Objective Met

Like nearly all other major Allied units, the 3rd Canadian Division failed to reach any of its D-Day objectives — with one exception. One troop of C Squadron, 1st Hussars, managed to get to the Caen-Bayeux railway line. Lieutenant William F. McCormick led a group of tanks in support of the Royal Winnipeg Rifles. Engineers had worked to clear the obstacles blocking the exits from the beach. C Squadron was able to pass over a precarious makeshift bridge that included a toppled truck and to gain access to the road. Although the beach was by no means quiet and enemy machine-gun fire and sniper fire occasionally rang out, the tanks encountered little opposition and "that's why we got so far inland," recalled McCormick. The tanks pushed through to Cruelly and on through lighter fire into Camilly. "We just kept on going…. We shot up a German scout car and inflicted some German infantry casualties. I was even saluted by a German soldier. I guess he was surprised to meet us so far inland."

(Left) Lieutenant William McCormick, center, and his crew from the 1st Hussars beside their Sherman tank.

THE WESTERNMOST BRITISH BEACH WAS CODE-NAMED GOLD AND ASSIGNED TO MAJOR GENERAL
D. A. H. Graham's 50th (Northumbrian) Division. Its tasks included capturing Bayeux on
the Anglo-American army boundary and linking up with the Americans on their right.
The 8th Armoured Brigade provided a screen of DD tanks for the 231st and 69th Brigades,
with the 151st Brigade as divisional reserve. Also going ashore at Gold with the first
wave was 47 Royal Marine Commando — a special-service unit with orders to strike eastward across the gap between Gold and Omaha to contact the Americans and dominate
the gap between the two armies. (The 48 and 41 Commandos performed similar linking
services between the Canadians and British to the east.)

   Like their American colleagues at Omaha, many RAF aircraft had dropped their bombs
too far inland of Gold — and German resistance here was stiffer than on Sword or Juno.

(Below) The wide low beaches of Gold
today, and (inset) as they looked on June 6,
1944. The smoke in the air is most likely
from burning tanks. (Opposite) A British
tank rolls ashore at Gold unmolested.

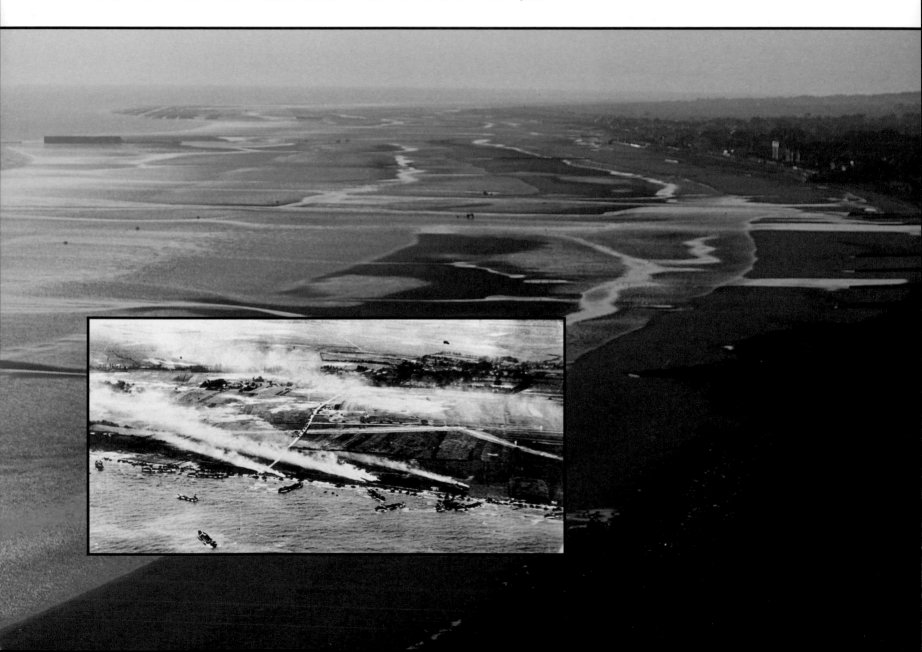

Trooper Ronald Mole of C Squadron, 4th/7th Royal Dragoon Guards, was the gunner–wireless operator on a DD tank that ran ashore at 0718. He remembered how another tank was literally hoisted by its own petard when a much-feared German 88-mm gun scored a direct hit on a vehicle carrying a ton of dynamite for demolitions:

> There was an AVRE, a Churchill [tank]. Now this was what they called a "petard." It had a shortish, wide barrel, which fired a forty-pound charge of dynamite, obviously a blockbuster. This thing came up and passed us and I'm watching [it] going on in front. It had got about fifty feet up the beach when suddenly there was a flash and sixty tons of metal just disappeared in front of your eyes. Then down came a sprocket, a piece of track, flames licking on the sand: a whole Churchill tank literally disappeared in front of your eyes.

MEDICAL ORDERLY GEOFFREY HAYWARD OF THE RAMC HAD A MACABRE EXPERIENCE OF HIS own soon after landing at Gold, when he and a friend took a look inside an abandoned German bunker:

> It was in half-darkness. There was [a machine gun] on the floor on its stand. I walked round that and past it — you don't touch anything in case it's mined, you see — toward the end of the bunker and my eyes got used to the [lack of] light, and there was a man lying on a trestle at the end. I went a bit closer and he was a very tall blond man, very good-looking, about thirty-five.... He was dressed in evening dress and he had a red carnation... attached to his jacket. And there he lay, quite rigid, on this thing. I counted eleven bullet holes in his chest. I should think some of the boys must have...found him in there and just killed him.

Bringing in the Troops at Gold

Gunner's Mate John P. Cummer (left) of the USS *LCI(L)-502* recalls the hazardous job of landing 196 members of the Durham Light Infantry at Gold Beach:

"The noise, smoke and confusion grew as we threaded our way through a mass of wrecked landing craft, tanks and beach obstacles. The nice, tight directions of our group commander as to our order of landing disappeared, as the confusion of the beach made it totally impossible. It was every ship for itself.... At one point, close to shore, our bow was aimed directly at a sunken truck with two wet, forlorn-looking soldiers clinging to it [opposite, top inset]. At the last moment, we changed course to avoid them. With a look of great relief on their faces, they waved to us as we lurched past them on our way to the rather improbable landing spot our Skipper had chosen out of necessity — a broached British LCT."

"The nice, tight directions of our group commander as to our order of
landing disappeared.... It was every ship for itself."

— Gunner's Mate John P. Cummer, USN

(Above) A panoramic shot of Gold
Beach on the morning of June 6, as
large landing craft bring in more British
troops. By this time, initial German
resistance has been overcome. Most of
the first waves of troops have moved
inland. (Inset, top) Two British soldiers
sit stranded on their sunken vehicle.
(Inset, bottom) By low tide, the beach
was scattered with empty landing craft
and abandoned vehicles.

Moving out from Gold

Twenty-six-year-old Bill Cheall (above), a seasoned soldier with the 6th Green Howards, noticed a change in the makeup of the countryside as they advanced from Gold Beach:

"We were confronted by a situation we had not seen before. It was called the bocage — small fields which all had V-shaped ditches around them. The earth from the ditches formed a bank and on top of the banks, hedgerows had been planted. It was ideal country for defensive positions to be set up, but disadvantageous to attackers. We met stubborn resistance about three miles inland. The enemy were putting down intensive machine-gun fire from a small wood and we could not get around it. Then we saw something new to us — the CO had got a message over the air with the result that a Churchill tank came up in no time at all. It went toward the wood and came under antitank fire, whereupon it retaliated quick as a flash. It was a flame-throwing tank and it shot a huge tongue of flame toward the wood and fried the enemy who had been holding us up...."

AN IMPORTANT OBJECTIVE FOR THE 50TH DIVISION WAS THE COASTAL VILLAGE OF ARROMANCHES-les-Bains to the right (west) of Gold Beach. One of the two Mulberry artificial harbors was to be set up there and it had to be well protected from a German attack from inland. (The imposing remains of this extraordinary achievement can still be seen sixty years later.) Lieutenant Colonel Donald May of the Royal Engineers' Port Construction Unit had helped assemble the components near Beachy Head on the south coast of England. He and his men sailed direct to Arromanches as soon as the shoreline was secure. Great floating concrete caissons were towed into place by some two hundred tugs. Blockships were used to close gaps between the caissons. Piers and floating roadways were assembled from chains of barges linked by bridges to each other and the shore. May went ashore for a meeting with senior officers:

> *We were walking along the prom to where we thought the meeting was going to be, and we heard some foreign language being spoken. [Brigadier] Waters said, "That isn't French, it isn't English: I'll see who they are." He went to this café, which was on the side, and came out with three fellows in front of him. He had his pistol in his hand and they had their hands up, and he took them over to the seawall and they stood there, and he came and said, "Donald, have you got any cartridges in your bloody gun? Mine is empty."*

(Above) British Centaur and Sherman tanks roll inland from the King Green sector of Gold Beach.

D-DAY ENDED WITH SOME 23,000 AIRBORNE AND OVER 130,000 seaborne troops in five beachheads on the shores of northwestern France. An outstanding achievement — even though no major Allied unit reached the optimistic day-one objective-line on Montgomery's campaign map. (The Americans from Utah were nearest; those at Omaha, farthest.) It was not yet a united bridgehead. But the Germans had failed to hurl the invaders back into the sea, and their divided command was already throwing units into the line piecemeal.

Casualty figures (killed, wounded or captured) on the first day of the Normandy campaign — although very hard to extricate from the figures for the eighty days of the complete campaign — touched five figures and were distinctly higher than German losses on day one. (The advantage always lies with the defenders when an invasion begins.) Yet losses were low in the most vulnerable phase of Overlord — well below ten percent. The Americans, with the special problems of their airborne and Omaha operations, lost over six thousand men, while the British may have lost half as many and the Canadians about one thousand. D-Day ended with the outcome finely balanced.

(Above) Mesmerized crowds outside *The New York Times* building in Manhattan follow the unfolding story of the invasion on the paper's outdoor headline-display board. (Right) Newspapers everywhere trumpeted the invasion, giving it front-page coverage.

The Hardest Part Was the Waiting. . . .

War bride Jean Imrie Deshane (inset) was stationed with the Auxiliary Territorial Service (ATS, a women's reserve branch of the British army) in Gateshead-on-Tyne, England:

"We all knew D-Day was coming but it had been talked about for so long, we had gotten complacent. I think those of us involved with men who were going to take part indulged in reverse thinking: 'Yes, we can't wait to start the freedom attempt, but maybe my man won't have to be there!' My fiancé had just had a leave in May and we had talked about our upcoming wedding. On June 6 when we reported for work, as the major was going into his office, he turned and said, 'I suppose you all know by now that we landed in Normandy this morning.' He then looked at me and said, 'Sit down, Imrie — he'll be back.' It was two long weeks before any mail came through, and every morning the thought was the same: 'I wonder if Carm is still alive?' He landed on Juno Beach at 11 A.M. on June 6 as a sniper with the 3rd Canadian Division. And he did make it back, thank God."

(Right) Jean Imrie and Carman Deshane on their wedding day in January 1945.

The Mulberry Artificial Harbors

From the town of Arromanches today, the scattered concrete remains of Mulberry Harbor B are still visible. Although battered and half-buried in the sand, their sheer size is still impressive. But then, almost everything about the Mulberries was impressive — two artificial harbors the size of Dover, constructed by the Allies on the spot in Normandy in a matter of days (and sometimes even under fire).

On D-Day itself, the initial stages — the Gooseberries, long breakwaters consisting of old merchant ships — were being sailed into place and scuttled. These were soon supplemented by the enormous Phoenixes — gargantuan barges several stories high sunk to extend the breakwaters and provide shelter for larger ships. After that came a succession of oddly named wonders: Bombardons, unique floating breakwaters; Whales, roads running over concrete floats called Beetles; and Spudheads, floating piers attached to enormous pillars set on the sea bottom.

Assembling the Mulberries was a complicated business that had to be planned in advance very carefully. And hauling the various components across the Channel was a round-the-clock effort. Each night four or five Phoenixes, six Bombardons and various other floating pier heads or parts of roads set sail. Not that the Allies waited until the Mulberries were fully assembled to start using them. Almost from the moment the first Gooseberries settled into the sand, ships were unloading behind them, protected from the rough waters of the Channel.

(Above) The Mulberry harbor at Arromanches in full swing, 1944. (Opposite) The ruins of the harbor can still be seen today. A line of Phoenix breakwaters stretches out from the shore, while smaller Beetle floats are scattered along the beach in the foreground. (Opposite, inset) A tank moves along one of the Whale floating roads. (Below, left) Engineers complete the exit from one of the floating Whale roadways to dry land. (Below, right) The same location in Arromanches today.

CHAPTER NINE

The Gathering Standoff

"[Major General Clarence R. Huebner, CG US 1st Infantry] was impatient to clean up the beachhead that he might drive inland and secure his immediate objectives. 'It'll take time and ammunition,' I told him, 'perhaps more than we reckon on both.'"

— Lieutenant General Omar N. Bradley, June 7

■ ON JUNE 8, THE GERMAN SECURITY SERVICE (SD) completed a secret report detailing public reaction to the invasion. Trust in Field Marshal Rommel was high, it stated, and:

> The arrival of the invasion was generally seen as a relief from unbearable tension and oppressive uncertainty. It formed almost the sole subject of conversation.... [It] was received in part with great enthusiasm. It came as a great surprise for the many who, thanks to its prolonged absence, no longer believed in it. The mood has changed at a stroke and is certainly serious about what is coming but very calm and confident. The reports on the progress of the battles on the Atlantic [coast] are being followed with much excitement.... The vast majority of people now believe that the invasion will decide the outcome of this war and that an end of the entire war is not too far off.... Only a few people purport to see the operations just begun as a feint rather than the decisive event.

NORMANDY: D-DAY + 7

(Previous page) A British tank belonging to the 13/18th Hussars pauses near Ranville on June 7, 1944. Gliders from the airborne assault lie scattered across the fields as smoke from a small battle rises in the distance. (Inset) After the invasion, the Germans raced to shore up their positions behind the Allied beaches. Here, a German self-propelled gun from the 21st Panzer Division passes the wing of a wrecked British glider sometime on June 7.

(Left) By the end of June 6, 1944, the Allies had a firm hold on their beachheads all across Normandy. Within a week, these disparate toeholds had been melded into one unified bridgehead — but the Allies had still failed to take many of their early objectives. (Opposite, top) Wehrmacht armored units in Normandy. The presence of the German 21st Panzer Division came as a surprise to the Allies. The subsequent arrival of more armored units helped slow down the Allied advance even further. (Opposite, bottom) A "Firefly" — a Sherman tank equipped with a heavy 17-pounder gun for attacking other tanks — on the move to counter the German armored threat.

HITLER AND MOST OF HIS COMMANDERS, ON THE OTHER HAND, BELIEVED THAT THE NORMANDY landings — despite their massive scale — were a diversion to draw attention away from the Pas de Calais. This was just as the Allied disinformation strategy had intended. But that intelligence success was significantly undermined by the failure to register the 21st Panzer Division's presence in the Caen area. The result was a protracted stalemate

"We nudge our way from cover to cover, ready for any enemy patrol which might be a target...."

— SS-*Obersturmführer* Peter Hansmann, 12th SS Panzer Division

around that city. The Canadians also failed to take Carpiquet Airfield quickly, to the west of the city — all of which gave Rommel (who raced back to France on the afternoon of D-Day) a welcome breather. The 12th SS Panzer Division launched its counterattack against the Canadians on June 7, which stabilized the front along the main road from Caen to Bayeux.

But Bayeux itself, on the boundary line between the two Allied armies, was the first French city to be liberated on June 7 by troops of the XXX British Corps. The 50th Division linked up with the American 1st Division, which had driven back the 352nd German Division from Omaha, at Port-en-Bessin (northwest of Bayeux) late on the eighth. The five Allied beachheads and the flanks seized by the three airborne divisions now constituted a continuous bridgehead some sixty miles wide — though not as strong or as deep as the generals would have liked.

The follow-up formations came pouring in over the beaches. The British airborne and their commando and infantry reinforcements were hanging on while the 3rd Division of the I British Corps was still held up by the guns and tanks of the 21st Panzer at Lébisey Wood just north of Caen. Congestion on both Sword and Gold delayed the tanks the British desperately needed to move forward — and also prevented more from landing. The Canadians were in no better shape on Juno. The bad weather, which had returned after the relative calm of D-Day, only added to the chaos.

The crack Panzer Lehr Division, commanded by Lieutenant General Fritz Bayerlein, was needlessly exposed to RAF fighter-bombers when it was ordered to move north by daylight to block a British advance on the village of Villers-Bocage. The fighter-bombers were known to German troops — who hated them especially — as *Jabos* (*Jagdbomber*, or hunter-bombers). They attacked any German vehicle that moved by road or rail, forcing the defenders to move by night — when the French Resistance sabotaged their trains or the tracks. Even so, Panzer Lehr denied the place to the XXX Corps.

There could be no question of a heavy and concerted counterattack, especially since Hitler had forbidden any withdrawal. Montgomery therefore decided on a pincer attack on Caen from east and west — but had to contend with a local counterattack on June 10, which took two hard days to fend off.

A counter-counterattack by a few tanks and troops from the 6th Airborne to the east after dark on the twelfth staved off defeat. On that day, SS General Sepp Dietrich — commander of the I SS Panzer Corps and an old-guard Nazi street-fighter turned tank general — took over the defense of Caen. He held off the pincer attacks by the freshly landed 51st Highland Division from the east and the 7th "Desert Rats" Armoured Division (Major General G. W. E. J. Erskine) from the west. Panzer Lehr also tied down the 50th Division. Meanwhile, the undetected and unbombed 2nd Panzer Division moved up in support all the way from Amiens to defend Villers-Bocage — which soon became the scene of a British debacle.

(Opposite) A street in the medieval city of Bayeux today and (inset) as it looked in June 1944. Bayeux sustained relatively little damage when it fell to the Allies on June 7. The British army would have its headquarters here for some weeks to come.

"What Kind of War Was This?"

As a beach commando with the Royal Canadian Navy, W. K. "Bill" Newell (left) assisted with the traffic on Juno Beach, including the transportation of POWs and casualties:

"One of the wounded stood up, disdainful of being assisted, and I could see that he wore a German uniform, with his left arm missing below the shoulder.... He jumped down from the six-foot height and fell in front of me. I reached down to help him up and he shook me off, standing up on his own. He was a very young, blond soldier and he stood very close to me, staring into my eyes. He was no more than fifteen years old, staring into the eyes of an eighteen-year-old. He spit in my face, and turned and walked up the ship's ramp. My emotion turned in a flash from one of sympathy to one I couldn't name, and my first impulse was to shoot him. [Then I] lowered my weapon and just stood there shaking my head.... What kind of war was this?"

The Balloon Soldiers

The 39ers Invasion Group (below, in July 1944) were part of the 320th AA Barrage Balloon Battalion, VLA. In the still-segregated American army, they were the only African-American combat unit included among the first assault forces to hit Normandy. Intended to thwart air attacks, barrage balloons flew from landing craft as they crossed the Channel during the first days of the invasion. Later they protected the beaches while their operators hunkered down in foxholes or former German pillboxes. Sergeant George Davison (back row, left) wrote to his wife from France on June 14:

"I am in good health and condition.... There was not a moment that I was not thinking about everyone back home. All sorts of thoughts came through my mind. After I had secured myself firmly in the ground like a groundhog, I felt a little bit better.... Write me and tell me what went on in the States and at home on the day of the invasion. Well, ours was a day of ducking bullets and anything [else] that could kill a man."

(Opposite) A steady procession of trucks leaves two American LSTs sitting high and dry on Omaha Beach at low tide. (Right) Canadian tanks and trucks come ashore at Juno Beach, protected from air attacks by barrage balloons flying overhead. Although there was little chance of German air attacks in the days after the landings, the beaches were still within range of artillery for several days.

The Road out of Omaha

Sergeant Henry Doar (inset, left) claimed his "fifteen minutes of fame" in the now-famous photograph (above right) of the 2nd Infantry Division filing past a captured German gun emplacement at Omaha Beach on June 7: "On D-Day+1, after coming back to the beach to look for my company in the 9th Infantry Regiment, I joined a unit of the 2nd coming up the bluff.... As I walked, I heard someone say 'Hey, Sergeant!' I looked up and an AP photographer I had met earlier took a picture." In 1946, the AP sent Henry Doar the photo and a letter. The letter has since been lost but Doar still has the original photo. Although many soldiers have claimed to be the man looking at the camera, Doar firmly stands by his story — and by his photograph. (Above left) Before this German battery was knocked out and taken over as a U.S. command post, its guns inflicted heavy damage on, among others, bulldozer operators from the 37th and 149th Combat Engineers during D-Day. Two of the operators were awarded the Distinguished Service Cross for heroically clearing a road out of Omaha while under intense fire. (Left) The battery stands today as a memorial.

(Below) Shattered British tracked vehicles and a charred six-pounder gun line the road outside Villers-Bocage. (Bottom, left) German troops examine a disabled British Firefly tank. (Bottom, right) A ravaged Cromwell tank inside the town. When the Cromwell was hit by an 88-mm shell fired by Panzer ace Michael Wittmann, tank commander Captain Pat Dyas was blown clear out of the vehicle — but escaped with his life. Three other members of his crew were not as lucky.

VILLERS-BOCAGE WAS AT THE JUNCTION OF SEVERAL ROADS AND THUS CRUCIAL FOR CONTROL OF the area southwest of Caen. The 7th Armoured Division was ordered to move around the right flank of the 50th Division to deliver a "right hook" against the village. The 22nd Armoured Brigade, led by Brigadier Robert Hinde — a dashing tank commander in the classic mold (unhelmeted head with beret and earphones protruding from the turret of a leading tank) — led the attack from the north on the afternoon of June 12. It was the first major British move into the bocage. When the brigade surged into the village early on the thirteenth, local people gave the soldiers an overwhelming welcome. Hinde also occupied the high ground to the northeast, on the main road to Caen.

So far, so good. But just outside the town to the south were two reserve companies of the I SS Panzer Corps. One of them was Number 2 Company of the 501st Heavy Tank Battalion, which, after suffering losses to air attacks, fielded five Mark VI E tanks — the world's most powerful at the time. These fifty-six-ton "Tigers" could outgun every Allied tank and, heavily armored, were hellishly difficult to knock out. The company was commanded by SS Lieutenant (later Captain) Michael Wittmann, the world's leading tank "ace" — who boasted a scarcely credible record of destruction on the Russian front (117 tanks) and the rare Knight's Cross with Oak Leaves at his collar. He was thirty years old.

To probe southward deeper into the bocage, Hinde sent the 4th Battalion, County of London Yeomanry (known as the Sharpshooters and equipped with obsolescent Cromwell tanks), followed by a company of motorized infantry from the 1st Battalion of

The Landscape of War

Eighteen-year-old Leslie Dinning (below), a member of the 4th County of London Yeomanry and later the 1st Royal Tank Regiment — both part of the famed Desert Rats — landed with the Yeomanry's Recce (reconnaissance) Troop at Gold Beach on D+1. As the men moved inland, Dinning took every opportunity to explore:

"There was a great deal of damage to property and farm stock…. There were a lot of dead cows in the fields, and quite a few dead German soldiers who had not yet been buried. The smell was horrible, but one got used to it. I think!… It was fortunate for me that I was reserve crew, because on June 13 the regiment was leading the division in a break through the German lines and during a major battle at Villers-Bocage, the Regimental Headquarters, A Squadron and Recce Troop were destroyed."

the Rifle Brigade. When the twenty-five British tracked vehicles stopped on a sunken, hedge-lined road to await further orders, some crews dismounted for a tea break. Wittmann, who had seen them coming, was lurking behind hedges in a field a quarter of a mile from the road. He took his tank down a parallel cart track, got ahead of the British column, turned through a gap in the hedge and disabled its leading tank with a single 88-mm round from eighty yards. The road was now blocked. It was also too narrow for the British vehicles to turn around between the impenetrable hedgerows.

In the deadly confusion that followed, British communications broke down — in large measure because it was impossible for the British infantry to communicate directly with tank crews. (Panzers had a telephone at the back for this purpose, an idea copied by the Americans.) And tapping on several inches of armor plate amid the pandemonium of battle was useless.

Wittmann drove along the paralyzed British column and coolly shot up one halftrack or tank after another through the hedges in a five-minute swathe of destruction — surely the greatest damage ever done by a single tank in a single engagement. Then he brought up the rest of his truncated company, which collectively destroyed twenty-five British tanks and nearly thirty other vehicles of the 22nd Brigade. (In a later attack Wittmann lost four tanks to British fire, including his own, but he lived to fight another day.) The two lead units of the 22nd Brigade were effectively destroyed and the rest withdrew.

After the loss of more than sixty tanks and hundreds of vehicles, General G. C. Bucknall of the XXX Corps ordered the 7th Division to withdraw. The 2nd Panzer attacked the rest of Hinde's brigade — which, after some support from American artillery firing at long range from the west, withdrew on the night of June 14. The Germans reoccupied Villers-Bocage and stayed there, despite a heavy RAF raid that all but destroyed the village. The "right hook" thus turned into a pulled punch — a disaster for the British army and its campaign plan.

Wittmann had plugged the temporary gap in the German line between the 2nd Panzer and Panzer Lehr — halting the British 2nd Army in its tracks. He was killed near Falaise on August 8, 1944, when his unsupported Tiger took on five Canadian Shermans in a single engagement. His final personal score was 138 tanks destroyed.

HAVING FAILED IN HIS FRONTAL ATTACK ON CAEN AND THEN WITH HIS PINCER MOVEMENTS ON Caen and Villers-Bocage, Montgomery rationalized the resulting stalemate. The planned swift capture of Caen was transformed into a strategy of drawing the main German armored formations onto the 2nd Army so that Bradley's 1st Army could break out on the right of the British. Historians have argued about Montgomery's Normandy strategy ever since, but his own draft plans show that he originally meant to take Caen on day one and move the Allied front steadily southward across Normandy. Before mid-June 1944, he gave no hint that he intended Caen to be the hinge of his campaign. Eisenhower was expecting a breakout on the (British) left — the short route to Paris — as much as on the American

(Above) A disabled Tiger tank — perhaps from Michael Wittmann's unit — stands at the edge of a large bomb crater amid the ruins of Villers-Bocage. The Germans reoccupied the town on June 14 and held on despite a devastating bombing campaign by the RAF.

right, and was bitterly frustrated by the developing and essentially pointless siege of Caen.

One obvious weakness in the "plan" to hold down the Germans was that the more of them the British attracted, the harder it would be to overcome them — although this approach, along with unrelenting air harassment, did prevent a massed enemy counterattack. Even if Montgomery was unable to dislodge the four panzer divisions in the Caen area, he could have sealed off the city and moved on — as did the Americans with strongpoints in the Pacific, and the Russians during their westward advance. Instead the British mounted three offensives, each bigger than the last, against the capital of Normandy — which was eighty-six percent destroyed in the process. Thanks to some unfathomable quirk in a staff officer's mind, the operations were all named after English racecourses: "Epsom," "Charnwood" and, finally, "Goodwood."

TWO WEEKS AFTER D-DAY, THE ALLIES HAD TWENTY DIVISIONS IN NORMANDY — HALF A million men. On June 19, a three-day storm in the Channel delayed the arrival of tens of thousands more men and masses of supplies. Eight hundred ships were sunk, damaged or beached. (It is worth noting that June 19 had been the fallback date for the invasion. In such appalling weather, the operation would undoubtedly have been cancelled altogether.) The start of "Epsom" was delayed by six days, to June 26. Lieutenant General Sir Richard O'Connor's VIII Corps led the XXX and I Corps in an attack west of Caen toward the river Odon, which flows northeastward into the city. The Allies knew that the 1st SS Panzer Division was on its way. They needed to attack the three armored divisions already there (21st, Lehr and 12th SS) before it joined them.

(Below, left) War artist Dwight Shepler documented the fierce storm of June 19–22, 1944, as heavy seas pounded the sunken blockships (code-named Gooseberries) that made up part of the massive Mulberry artificial harbor at Omaha Beach.
(Below) The aftermath of the storm.

Bad weather deprived the VIII Corps of air cover as the British pushed the Germans (led by SS General Dietrich) back toward the river Odon in intense fighting in the bocage. An almighty struggle for an unremarkable hill near Maltot — a village southwest of Caen between the rivers Odon and Orne — became the decisive engagement. In its level of pointless to-and-fro attrition, it was reminiscent of the First World War.

RIFLEMAN NORMAN HABETIN WAS A RADIO OPERATOR WITH THE MOTORIZED 8TH BATTALION of the Rifle Brigade, serving with the 11th Armoured Division. A little the worse for wear from drinking "liberated" Calvados (the notorious local brandy distilled from cider), Habetin and his unit approached Maltot from the west on the afternoon of June 26, after a confused and bloody action near Cheux village. They came under heavy mortar fire and took cover:

> *Eventually the mortaring stopped. Then we got up [and there was] total chaos. Nobody knew what the hell was happening.... There was a small hill nearby. Actually, this hill became one of the most notorious hills of the whole campaign. It was called Hill 112.... Our carrier was ordered to the top of this*

(Opposite) A piper leads members of the 7th Seaforth Highlanders, 51st Highland Division, into action at the beginning of Operation Epsom. (Inset) A truck packed with ammunition explodes after being hit by enemy mortar fire as British armored units — part of the XXX Corps — advance during Operation Epsom.

hill. We got to the top and dug this trench.... Then we started being mortared. This went on for the remainder of the day. There was nothing we could do.... This night turned into a kind of nightmare of tanks milling around in the dark, exploding mortars...and the expectation of a sudden enemy bayonet attack.... The Germans were all around us.... It was horrible up there. We were overlooking Caen, which we could see clearly, and a place called Carpiquet Aerodrome.

(Above) Tanks belonging to Britain's 23rd Hussars advance on the river Odon during Operation Epsom. (Below) Tracked troop carriers bearing members of the 8th Battalion of the Rifle Brigade, covered by tanks from the 23rd Hussars, mass at the foot of Hill 112.

But Habetin and his battalion managed to escape with relatively minor casualties at 3 A.M. on June 27.

Another participant in the long battle for Hill 112 was Herbert Fürbringer of the 19th Panzer-Grenadier Regiment, ordered out of shattered Caen by the II SS Panzer Corps to join the fight on the twenty-seventh. Various German tank and motorized-infantry units in their turn occupied part of the hill with heavy losses in the dark. Fürbringer was acting as runner for SS Captain Bruno Kriz, commanding Number 3 Company of the regiment's 1st Battalion. Fürbringer was the only survivor of two separate detachments destroyed in the action, and was therefore nicknamed "Feuerfest" (Fireproof) Fürbringer. Kriz gathered the remnants of his unit together — some eighty men — and sent Fürbringer up the hill, alone, to find out what was happening:

The night became day. Every German fought silently and bitterly. The enemy defensive fire was frightful. The noise of battle grew quiet in the morning hours. The artillery was silent.... Radio and telephone were shut down. What

"The sparks flew. We had been hit from the right.... A hair's-breadth in front of our panzer, armor-piercing solid shot was tearing horrible black furrows in the green grass."

— SS-*Scharführer* Willy Kretschmar, 12th SS Panzer Regiment, near Hill 112

was going on up top? That was our fearful question. Hill 112 was a bloody merry-go-round. How much longer would it go on turning? What had happened to our two battlegroups? Why did no wounded men come back?

As Fürbringer came alongside a panzer, it came under fire from British guns:

Before the tank commander shut the hatch, he shouted to me to take cover under the tank. Shrapnel buzzed, clattered and hammered on the steel of the tank with such effect on my morale that I never took shelter under a tank again. Even so, I got to the top of the hill unhurt. What met my eyes there was unimaginable. Masses of dead, friend and foe alike, lay scattered on the flat ground in front of a copse and a cattle enclosure.

The Germans attacked the 5th Dorsets in the afternoon, even before the German preparatory bombardment ended. The British guns were firing back:

We were spared nothing. The air was full of flying steel and smoke — and the stench of decay from the fallen. The thermometer showed a temperature of thirty degrees [Celsius]; there was scarcely the tiniest cloud in the sky. We always had to reckon with attack fighters.

Eventually even Fürbringer could not live up to his nickname:

A heavy blow hit my right leg. My camouflage uniform hung in shreds. I had five shell splinters in my thigh and calf.

He managed to limp to a dressing station down the hill. Kriz and his unit were wiped out by nightfall as the first German counterattack was beaten off on the twenty-seventh. Once again Fürbringer, though no longer fireproof, was a lone survivor. The Germans mounted another counterattack on the twenty-ninth and finally drove off the British. They remained in possession of Hill 112 on July 1. Epsom had been called off the previous day, when Montgomery decided to cut his considerable losses — especially infantry, for whom there were alarmingly few replacements in war-weary Britain. Caen had not been outflanked from the west. More by luck than judgment, the mutual attrition managed to deprive the Germans of their chance of a mass armored counterattack just as the 9th and 10th SS Panzer Divisions arrived from the Russian front.

But the British 2nd Army was also stopped. Short of the abundant manpower available to the Americans, it had to content itself with a series of pulled punches for much of the remaining campaign. To keep fighting divisions up to strength, Montgomery was forced to raid two divisions, which disappeared completely from the order of battle. Mysteriously, however, there were more infantrymen still in Britain than in Montgomery's entire Army Group. Perhaps the War Office was merely incompetent; or perhaps the British government wanted to minimize losses in the last phase of the war.

The Human Face of Battle

Sydney Jary (above) took over as commander of 18 Platoon, D Company, 4th Battalion, the Somerset Light Infantry, on July 31 after the regiment suffered terrible casualties at Hill 112 and Briquessard. He recalls coming upon a slit trench, surrounded by churned-up earth, in what remained of the garden of a small French cottage near Eterville not far from Hill 112:

"The trench was unoccupied but traces of its previous occupants lay all around. A gas cape, wet with the morning dew. Clips of .303 cartridges were on the parapet.... In the bottom of the trench lay a cluster of thirty-six grenades, a large pool of blood and an unravelled shell dressing. None of these surprised me. [Then] my eyes rose, my throat tightened and tears came. Sitting on a tiny ledge cut into the side of the trench was a small, light brown teddy bear. He wore a red and white ribbon collar with a bell attached. I was just twenty years old and this was my introduction to battle."

For the Germans, stuck with Hitler's standing "no retreat" order, it was an article of faith that the best form of defense was attack. For the British, the attack on Normandy had become defensive. As inter-Allied tensions rose in the Normandy stalemate, the Americans accused Montgomery of being too cautious. But one of Montgomery's great virtues as a general trained on the western front of the First World War was his extreme reluctance to waste lives. He now had to live with the uncomfortable and oft-proved fact that, man for man, German first-line troops were superior to his own — whether British, Canadian or American. Only greater numbers and firepower would ensure victory. That, and German command blunders.

FOR OPERATION CHARNWOOD, MONTGOMERY ENLISTED THE RELUCTANT SUPPORT OF THE ALLIED strategic bomber forces for a massive preliminary bombardment of the Caen area. Eisenhower, still in England, backed him because he wanted some real progress on the left wing. At the end of the first week in July, the I British Corps and Canadian troops managed to seize (at high cost to both sides) northern Caen as far as the north bank of the Orne — although the area south of the river remained in German hands. The Carpiquet airfield fell at last into Allied hands.

(Above) Signaling the start of Operation Charnwood, 450 British heavy bombers pound Caen during a daylight attack late on July 7. (Below) Canadian artillery fire on the city in preparation for the infantry attack. (Opposite) Canadian war artist Orville Fisher depicted the capture of the battered Carpiquet airfield by soldiers from the 3rd Canadian Division on July 8.

The Bombing of Caen

Second Lieutenant Ken Davenport (above) was with the 5th Battalion, the King's Regiment (Liverpool), in Normandy and remembers the devastating bombing of Caen:

"The first time I went into [the area close to] Caen, we did see these thousands of British bombers. They came overhead wave after wave after wave. We knew Caen was the target. A few days later, I suppose it would be, we moved up into Caen and one...perhaps unexpected memory out of all the killing and the shambles [was] that there was an arm sticking up out of the ruins with a golden wedding ring on it. It was a French civilian but I didn't know it at the time. That rather struck me forcibly what this war was all about."

Mrs. Simone Duncomb, a Frenchwoman who married a Briton after the war, was a twenty-year-old student in Caen in 1944 — a volunteer fighting fires and helping to tend the civilian wounded. The bombing forced the city's main hospital to seek refuge in a strange environment:

> We heard that the different sections of the hospital...were going to be moved outside of the center...to a village where there were mushroom caves. They were very damp. After very few days our clothes were all black with [mold]. Quite a few of us became ill after that, including myself. There were sick babies, newly born...also a lot of elderly people.... We had to help them, to nourish them, which was not always easy, because we had to go sometimes through the lines to get some food and it was very, very dangerous. A few of our team, friends, got wounded or died. There was even a birth in the cave.... Eighty children crying together in a damp atmosphere was [really] something....

As the troops and vehicles continued to pour into the choked British sector of the bridgehead, Hitler began to fire generals (a move some thought Montgomery should have copied sooner than he did). Rommel last saw his führer in Berlin on June 28 — eleven days after Hitler had made his sole visit to northern France — but failed to convince him of the seriousness of the situation there. On June 30, General Geyr von Schweppenburg of the newly formed Panzer Group West was replaced by General Hans Eberbach. Two days later, von Rundstedt (the supreme commander, west) "resigned" — an idea he got at dictation speed, by telephone from Berlin. He was relieved by Field Marshal Gunther von Kluge who, after an initial surge of confidence, soon joined the pessimist majority in the high command in France.

When Rommel was seriously wounded in his car by British fighters on July 17, von Kluge took over Army Group B as well. A few days earlier, Montgomery's old enemy from North Africa had tried, in a last letter, to awaken Hitler to the growing danger in France as the Allied armies grew remorselessly:

> Under these circumstances it must be reckoned that the enemy will succeed in the foreseeable future in breaking through our own meager front and break into broader French territory. The consequences will be incalculable. The troops are fighting heroically everywhere, but the unequal struggle is coming to an end. I must ask you to accept the consequences of this situation.

Hitler did no such thing. The newly unified command in France brought no relief from interference from Berlin. On the contrary. After the failure of the officers' bomb plot against Hitler on July 20, Rommel — indirectly implicated — was given the choice between trial for treason or a poison capsule. He chose the latter.

(Inset, left) Holed up in a house within the city, a British sniper watches for enemy movement. (Middle) Allied soldiers advance carefully through the rubble-strewn streets that the Germans had mined heavily before their retreat. (Right) Canadian soldiers crouch beside a roadmarker pointing toward Paris. Any hope of a fast breakout was lost in the weeks of fighting that followed. (Below) Allied trucks amid the rubble of Caen. More than eighty percent of the city was destroyed in the fight to secure it.

CHAPTER TEN

The Breakout

"They gave us about an hour's rest...and then we took off heading inland and we went like a bunch of bluetail flies."

— Captain John K. Slingluff, 29th Infantry Division, after clearing the bridgehead out of Omaha Beach

The thick hedges characteristic of the Normandy region made a great defensive feature that the Germans were quick to exploit. (Opposite) Hidden in the bocage, a camouflaged German antitank gun lies in wait. (Below) A German infantry patrol moves through the dense hedgerows.

THE AMERICANS WERE LATE TOO, according to General Montgomery. His plan of campaign had them on their start line for the breakout from the bridgehead on D+5 (June 11). But they did not get there until July 18 — more than five weeks later. "That fact is sometimes forgotten when the British army is criticized for not capturing Caen on D-Day or very soon after," he said in his retirement.

The Americans, however, had hardly been idle. By June 17, working westward from Utah Beach, they had cut off the northern half of the Cotentin Peninsula. On its northern coast was Cherbourg, a major port and an early objective of the invasion. By the end of the month, U.S. casualties (about thirty-four thousand) had surpassed Anglo-Canadian losses by well over nine thousand. The unexpectedly high infantry losses in the bocage were a problem for Bradley too — although it was not a question of finding manpower but of getting it into the front line quickly enough.

Having battered their way over the bluff and off Omaha Beach without significant armored or bombardment support — and at high cost — the Americans found themselves fighting Germans concealed in the bocage inland. Unprepared for the density and height of the accursed hedgerows, the Americans were driven to invent ad hoc methods of coping with them. High explosive was used to pierce them for the tank guns that targeted German heavy machine guns concealed in the corners of fields opposite farm gates and other gaps in the hedgerows. Major General J. Lawton "Lightning" Joe Collins of the VII Corps is credited with inventing the hedgebusting tank known as the "Rhinoceros." Lengths of rail were cut from Rommel's obstacles and welded onto the front of a tank to form an oversize "garden fork" that broke apart the hedgerows.

Eventually the Germans became victims of their own initial success in hampering the American landings. They began to run out of ammunition, especially for their artillery. No supplies were getting through to their fixed defenses along the shoreline, thanks to Allied airpower. The efforts of a multiplicity of units from the 352nd and static 709th Divisions to deny everything to the Americans eventually meant that the Germans lost

155

(Above) The ingenious Rhinoceros tank the Americans used to penetrate the bocage. (Opposite) Surviving hedgerows today outside the town of Colleville-sur-Mer. (Inset) An American infantry unit comes under heavy fire from snipers hidden in the trees and hedgerows along a country road in the Cotentin Peninsula.

everything. They sustained irreplaceable losses of manpower, many smaller units were isolated — and they could not concentrate their strength for the massive counterattack desired by Hitler and von Rundstedt.

For their part, the Americans seemed ready to attack everything at once with their superior firepower, numbers and supplies. Unfazed by the loss of their Mulberry off Omaha in the great storm of late June, they continued to pour vehicles and stores — as well as follow-up troops — across their beaches in huge numbers. Inexorable American pressure forced the right-wing boundary of the bridgehead southward and westward.

By the end of June, after the failure of Epsom and the limited success of Charnwood, it was clear to Montgomery that if there was going to be a breakthrough in the stalemate, it would have to be in the American sector. The Americans, with their greater freedom of movement, could concentrate their forces and punch a hole in the German containment line.

The British army, meanwhile, had defensively restricted itself to smaller probes and limited engagements in order to conserve its strength and retain the attention of the Germans, especially their armor, as Montgomery tried to make a virtue of necessity. Ironically, by making the best of a bad job in this way, the British c-in-c fell in neatly with Rommel's containment tactics of fighting for every foot of ground.

With a few gallant exceptions — such as General Gale of the 6th Airborne and General O'Connor of the VIII Corps — British generalship combined with indifferent training and poor equipment to produce lackluster results. The rank and file usually lacked personal initiative and tended to stop and wait for new orders if events did not go according to plan. There was a shortage of seasoned NCOs, the backbone of any army (the best ones had been promoted to lieutenant, a rank that suffered exceptionally high casualties). And British soldiers had not been trained for close-quarters fighting in wooded country, or for close cooperation between armor and infantry.

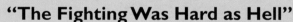

"The Fighting Was Hard as Hell"

Captain John K. Slingluff (left), Company G, 3rd Battalion, 175th Regiment, 29th Infantry Division, was wounded, then captured, while leading his men on a mission to secure and hold the bridges by the Vire Canal, thirteen miles inland:

"It looked to me as though we were fighting against the whole German army down in front of us.... A German mortar shell landed somewhere [near] me and sprinkled me a bit in the left knee and in the right hip. It stung, but it wasn't bad. I could see that we could not only not hold that position, but that we were going to be surrounded if I didn't do something quickly. So I had to order a retiring movement.... We were beginning to get thinned out pretty well, but we still had plenty of fight left in us. Then I was hit again. I got a rifle bullet that went through my right hip and that took all movement out of me.... We who were left behind continued to fight until we were about out of ammunition.... Colonel Goode stepped out and he surrendered us, and I became prisoner of war 80504 at that point."

Churchill was openly critical of Montgomery at a chiefs-of-staff meeting in London in the first week of July and had broadly hinted to Eisenhower (who did not have the right to dismiss a British officer) that should the supreme commander have misgivings about one — regardless of his rank — the prime minister would sanction his dismissal. Thanks to the stalemate and American impatience, Montgomery's position was certainly precarious, but he had a powerful friend at court — General Sir Alan Brooke, chief of the Imperial General Staff, who was indispensable to Churchill.

General Bradley was no less cautious strategically than Montgomery. In the days before Charnwood, his 1st Army launched a general southward attack across its entire front on July 3. But it petered out in the bocage in five days after only minor gains — which did not include the objective of St-Lô, a town on the Bayeux-Coutances highway and an important road junction. Panzer Lehr and the 2nd SS Panzer Divisions had moved westward to oppose the Americans in the west — although five panzer divisions remained on the stagnant British front, where the Allies faced nearly three times as many enemy tanks. After the American and British pushes had both stalled, Montgomery met his two army commanders, Dempsey and Bradley, on July 10. They planned coordinated attacks on both wings aimed at the longed-for and long-delayed breakout from the bridgehead. The results were Operation Goodwood for the British, and Operation Cobra for the Americans. Eisenhower and even the forever-bickering air commanders were enthusiastic.

General Patton, deeply contemptuous of Montgomery's caution and metaphorically pawing the ground like a stallion, was already in Normandy with the staff of his 3rd U.S. Army, about to be formed from freshly landed divisions. Patton's notorious trademark was a pair of pearl-handled Colt .45 revolvers in a Western-style gun belt; Montgomery's was a pair of regimental badges on his floppy beret. (Regulations forbade more than one badge, just as they forbade any weapon except those that were U.S. Army issue.) Both men instinctively understood that a general should be instantly — and, if necessary, idiosyncratically — recognizable to the troops. Patton's role was to exploit the breakout in the west promised by Bradley. He was only there on sufferance because Eisenhower desperately needed a pugnacious fighting general for this role. Patton had almost wrecked his career by publicly striking two soldiers with combat fatigue, and by publicly talking of American postwar domination. The liberal democracy he was fighting for was not his main preoccupation.

ON JULY 18, GENERAL DEMPSEY, 2ND ARMY COMMANDER (AND A FRUSTRATED MAN BECAUSE Montgomery would not delegate to him), inaugurated Operation Goodwood — a drive for the plain between Caen and Falaise, twenty-one miles to the southeast. More than twenty-six hundred tanks from three armored divisions and several independent armored brigades were involved, plus troops from four corps — three British (VIII, I and XII) and one Canadian (II). The assault was preceded by a heavy "softening-up" air bombardment, plus naval guns, plus artillery. But Montgomery had his misgivings, knowing full well

(Top) Major General Collins, left, accepts the surrender of Cherbourg from the German commander there. All resistance in the strategic port city and U-boat base ceased on June 27, 1944. (Above) Fourth of July celebrations bring a note of gaiety to Cherbourg after a month of grim fighting. (Below) Looking like a referee, General Bradley, center, stands between Generals Patton, left, and Montgomery, right, during a rare light moment between two men who heartily disliked each other.

that the Anglo-Canadians were better at defense than attack, that key units such as the 7th Armoured and 51st Highland Divisions were tired out and that his tanks were inferior to the Germans' — even though by now the Allies had a four-to-one advantage in numbers.

GENERAL HANS EBERBACH ASSUMED CONTROL OF THE GERMAN armored divisions in the recently formed Panzer Group West (soon to be restyled 5th Panzer Army) on July 13 and issued a special order of the day:

> I have taken over command…. We have reached the
> climax of this war. Our homeland, elderly workers and
> peasants, your mothers and wives, are working
> incredibly hard. They are doing it for you and in [their]
> belief in the necessity and success of this conflict. We do
> not want to let down this decent homeland: we want to
> oppose English [sic] material [superiority] with our
> German hearts until our victory. Heil Hitler!

Since his troops generally enjoyed the advantage of higher ground, they had detected a British armored buildup. Eberbach positioned elements of two corps to oppose the coming attack — four lines of defense, with a fifth in reserve. The first line was strong enough to force the British to stand and fight. But after that, it would withdraw on the much stronger second line. Once again the Allies would have to fight for every yard against a still-formidable enemy. Sergeant Kurflür, a tank commander in Number 4 Company, 22nd Panzer-Grenadier Regiment, took part in the ensuing battle and recalled the first Allied air raids of July 18:

> After the usual dispositions we were ready for sleep at
> 0530. I had already crawled underneath my tank when I
> suddenly heard the hum and roar of enemy air
> formations…. I don't think anyone was in his right mind
> after the first [bombing] wave. Three mates from my
> crew could not be held back. They ran off and I never saw
> them again. After the first wave we wanted to tidy up
> our camouflage but were soon reminded by attacking
> Jabos that none of us was to be allowed to live.

The hellish bombardment ended at about 9 A.M. The assembly area of the regiment, a hardy remnant of the 21st Panzer Division, was devastated:

> Several tanks had disappeared. The entire road had
> gone. Crater after crater made it almost impossible to
> find a way through. Yet it still proved possible to get
> six Mark IV tanks ready to start. With these tanks we
> moved to a new position around noon.

NORMAN HABETIN OF THE 8TH BATTALION, RIFLE BRIGADE, WAS NO less impressed by the barrage from air, sea and land. He and his mates agreed: "No one will ever survive that lot." They advanced in open order across a field behind a creeping barrage:

> But in amongst us enemy shells were bursting. We
> were all going along together in some kind of horrible
> devil's dance…. Then to my surprise I began seeing
> Germans all over the place, very much alive, running
> about. I thought to myself, "This is ridiculous.
> How the hell can people be alive after all this lot?"
> I couldn't believe it: they were.

After an advance of five miles, the battalion reached its first objective, the Caen-Paris railway line. The next day the riflemen were behind the 11th Armoured as it climbed Bourgébus Ridge, only to get stuck there when Dietrich of I SS Panzer Corps threw his last reserves into the largest armored battle of the Normandy campaign. Habetin had a clear view:

> The whole hillside was a horrible graveyard of
> burning tanks…. There were [German] 88s in the
> woods below, concealed. [The tanks] were just being
> topped off one after the other…. We realized there
> was no question of going further for anybody.
> Certainly not to Falaise…. That apparently was the
> end of this Goodwood attack. I think at that stage
> what was going on was that the British army was
> trying to attract most of the German army so that
> the Americans could nip out of the back door. I've
> learned this since. I didn't know that at the time.

Once again the 21st Panzer, assisted this time by the 16th Airborne Division, had frustrated the British, halting them before the 1st and then the 12th SS Panzer Divisions finally arrived to block the road to Falaise. The efforts of the 11th Armoured, the Guards Armoured and at the last the 7th Armoured Divisions, bogged down on cluttered roads, fizzled out by lunchtime on the eighteenth — not least because the infantry was held back instead of being used in close conjunction with the tanks. If General O'Connor of the VIII Corps had had his way, this would not have happened. But Montgomery held him back.

The 11th lost half its tanks (126); the Guards lost sixty. General Erskine kept the 7th out of harm's way and arrived late below the ridge, on top of which were the remains of the 1st SS Panzer Division. In the end, ground-attack fighters from the RAF prevented the Germans from forcing a British withdrawal from the slopes of the ridge. On the twentieth there was another rainstorm and thus no air support. Goodwood had run its course, into the mud — a less-than-brilliant advance of seven miles at a cost of over four hundred tanks.

Churchill was once again incensed by Montgomery's apparently incorrigible caution. Eisenhower was also extremely disappointed, and visited Montgomery to say so. Fortunately the Germans were too exhausted to indulge in their customary immediate counterattack. Meanwhile, the Canadians had taken control of the now-entirely-irrelevant Caen, apart from a few pockets of German resistance. But the German right wing was seriously weakened (though not yet broken) in a war of attrition that the enemy now knew he could not win.

MEANWHILE, AS A PRELIMINARY TO COBRA, MAJOR GENERAL CHARLES H. CORLETT'S XIX U.S. Corps had at last captured St-Lô on July 18. Collins's VII Corps now moved to an eastward position on the St-Lô–Periers road. Bradley's plan (strictly his own idea) was to break out of the bocage into open country to the south of the Cotentin, where American tanks would be able to exploit their superior numbers and speed, and head southward for the river Loire. Once again foul weather delayed the start from July 20 to the twenty-fifth; once again the Germans knew Bradley was preparing an attack. There were fewer than thirty thousand men of the German 7th Army to oppose him. Panzer Lehr was in the forefront.

But the Americans too called up massive air support as Bradley, for once, forbore from attacking all along his line. This time there was a concentrated thrust by the 30th and 9th Divisions — both of which suffered high casualties from their own side's airpower in a shattering bombardment. (The Army Air Force attacked across the American line instead of along and in front of its length, as Bradley had requested.)

The infantry managed to advance just two miles on day one, July 25. The next day, the VIII Corps (Major General Troy Middleton) came up alongside and on the right of the VII, which then renewed the attack, sending two armored columns forward. The Germans once again fought for every yard until the American 2nd Armored Division broke through

(Above) Infantry of the Stormont, Dundas and Glengarry Highlanders cross a Bailey bridge erected by Royal Canadian Engineers over the river Orne not far from Caen as part of Operation Atlantic — as the Canadian role in Goodwood was titled. (Below) American troops in the rubble-strewn streets of St-Lô during the costly offensive to take this key city on the western edge of the Cotentin Peninsula. (Bottom) The capture of St-Lô allowed the Americans to break through the German defenses and move out of Normandy.

Tragic Prelude to the Breakout at St-Lô

After receiving treatment for battle fatigue and minor wounds, Lieutenant Frank W. Towers (below) of the 120th Regiment, 30th Infantry Division, returned to his unit in time to participate in the St-Lô breakthrough:

"To assist in defining the bomb line [for the saturation bomb run] of the St-Lô–Periers highway, our artillery placed red smoke shells just south of the highway. Unfortunately, a slight breeze…caused the red smoke to slowly drift to the north, and directly over our troops in the front lines. Over 1,500 of the Air Corps' heavy bombers came over exactly on time and on course, and dropped their bombs right down on our troops, and as far back as the Regimental Headquarters."

With over 150 men killed or wounded, the attack was called off and rescheduled for the following day:

"…and again, same bomb line, same red smoke put out and, same breeze came up again! Right on time the 1,500 heavy bombers came over and dropped their load right down on the smoke line, which was again right on top of our troops…. Damage and casualties were beyond imagination! Bodies and wounded men were lying all around…."

Despite another 662 casualties, the attack went ahead on July 26 and by the end of the day, a wide breach had been made in the German defense lines.

(Above) American trucks roll through the ruins of St-Lô.

them at St-Gilles, on their right flank.

Bradley's objective of creating a three-mile gap — to be kept open by the two U.S. infantry divisions as armor and motorized infantry poured through — had at last been achieved. The pressure was off the VIII Corps, now placed under Patton, who was due to assume command of the 3rd U.S. Army on August 1 — with the order to break out at last. Four U.S. armored divisions raced southward from Coutances as SS panzer units fought a savage rearguard action with heavy casualties. The VIII Corps seized an undefended Avranches on July 30. The routes to the Loire, and to Brittany with its major ports to the west, were open.

After six days the American army was in open country — and Patton, with the XV Corps also under his command, was in the driver's seat. His orders were to secure Brittany and then turn east across France in a right hook toward Paris. For the first time in the campaign, Allied troops began to swallow up territory at almost breakneck speed as Patton — in his element as never before — led the charge. Montgomery, who thoroughly reciprocated Patton's dislike, was nevertheless hugely relieved and effectively tore up his plan for steady expansion of the bridgehead. He let Patton take the lead.

CHAPTER ELEVEN

Finale at Falaise

"Our basic plan of operation is to advance and to keep on advancing regardless of whether we have to go over, under or through the enemy."

— General George S. Patton

Spurred on by the breakout from Avranches on August 1, American tank forces race along roads and cut through fields lined with hedgerows on their way to Rennes a week later.

■ IN LESS THAN A WEEK, THE SITUATION in Normandy had been transformed from stalemate to breakthrough — as this report, dated July 27, 1944, makes unmistakably clear:

> *The Panzer Lehr Division, after forty-nine days of the hardest fighting, is destroyed with effect from today. Having broken through everywhere, the enemy is driving further southward from St-Gilles. All requests for help and reinforcements have so far gone unheeded because nobody believed how serious the situation is. Only insufficient and untrained forces were assigned to the division [during the campaign].*

It was sent to Field Marshal von Kluge, the supreme commander west, from one of the proudest units in the Wehrmacht. The words are those of Lieutenant General Fritz Bayerlein, the broken division's bitter and exhausted commander.

ON AUGUST 1, GENERAL BRADLEY BECAME COMMANDER OF A SEPARATE 12th Army Group — entirely American and consisting of the original 1st Army, now led by Lieutenant General Courtney Hodges, and Patton's 3rd Army. Eisenhower remained in England. The 1st Canadian Army (Lieutenant General H. D. G. Crerar) was formed from the II Canadian Corps and other units originally under the command of the 2nd British Army. The Canadians took over the eastern flank of the front as General Dempsey moved 2nd Army troops westward from the Caen area to Caumont — to link up with the American left in Operation Bluecoat, begun on July 30.

On the afternoon of August 1, the VIII U.S. Corps rumbled into Brittany. Its 4th Armored Division made for the capital, Rennes, while the 6th drove toward the major ports of St-Malo and Brest on its northern coast, plus Quiberon Bay to the south. Patton would brook no British-style delays. When a traffic jam built up in Avranches on the "corner" between Normandy and Brittany, he simply pushed his tanks through the town by force of personality — and by plain force where necessary. There was to be no cautious, step-by-step advance across the peninsula, which was to be held by relatively few troops while the bulk of the 3rd Army, led by the XV Corps, turned due east in the direction of Paris. Montgomery went so far as to advise the Americans not to waste time besieging

Brest at the western end of Brittany. The step-by-step strategy of Overlord was thrown overboard.

AS THE GERMAN POSITION IN FRANCE WORSENED, TENSION MOUNTED between the Wehrmacht (of which the German army was the major component) and the SS, whose fighting formations regarded themselves as a military elite — a belief encouraged by the fact that they had first call on all the best manpower and equipment. Lieutenant General Mahlmann wrote in his unpublished history of the 353rd Infantry Division in the Normandy campaign:

> *As a political fighting organization the SS was used to the gung-ho approach, but it obviously lacked the inexhaustible commitment, the silent devotion to duty which wins no laurels but which is always required of the army. The soldier at the front naturally asks why the SS is in so many respects better off than he is. The answer is that a distinction was made between Wehrmacht and party organization, in favor of the latter. Such a fact must have imposed a burden on the mental attitude of the ranks. Thus it is understandable that there were officers who tried hard to prevent this difference from being constantly paraded before their soldiers' eyes: so they tried to avoid mixing with the SS or [serving] next to them. A historian who wishes to explain the causes of the German collapse should not ignore such facts.*

Looking back on the campaign that turned irrevocably against the Germans in the first week of August, former SS officer Hubert Meyer made it clear that the disdain was mutual:

> *Unquestionably this battle was a serious defeat for the 5th German Panzer Army and the 7th Army, which suffered great losses in men and matériel in it. The cause is errors in leadership by the Wehrmacht supreme command.*

Hitler's constant interference in the campaign (another facet of the dictator's "divide and rule" approach) was the defenders' main problem. On August 2, he made what was probably his greatest mistake in the defense of Normandy when he ordered a horrified von

Kluge to use the battered 7th Army and Panzer Group West for a major counterattack northward toward Avranches and Mortain — with a view to dividing the Americans by cutting them off in the Cotentin and in Brittany. The hard-pressed German armor was ordered to pull back and regroup for this thrust — something it had been unable to do since June 6 and certainly could not afford to do now. Failure would mean that the Germans could be surrounded.

Nonetheless, on August 6, the 47th Panzer Corps — newly formed from the remnants of the 2nd Panzer, 1st SS and 2nd SS Panzer plus the newly arrived 116th Panzer Divisions — attacked the positions of the American 30th Division (Major General Leland S. Hobbs) east of Mortain; the 35th U.S. had just arrived at the town itself. Bradley received a brief warning of the impending attack from "Ultra," the priceless Allied intelligence derived from deciphering German signals. The assault, however — unheralded by the usual giveaway artillery barrage — achieved tactical surprise. As American and British fighter-bombers joined the fray (from which the Luftwaffe was entirely absent), a fierce struggle developed for a feature called Hill 317. In a classic, Alamo-style stand, the 2nd Battalion of the 120th Infantry Regiment, 30th Division, suffered forty percent casualties in holding on to the hill — a siege abandoned by the Germans only on August 12. The VII U.S. Corps got the upper hand over the attackers after a severe struggle.

In the unpublished history of the role of the 363rd Infantry Division in Normandy, Lieutenant General A. Dettling described how his division had covered the flank of General Eberbach's Panzer Group West in an attack toward Avranches on August 4. The next day the division replaced the indefatigable 21st Panzer and 116th Panzer in the Vire area, north of Mortain, where the Germans had already driven a salient into the American line. On the sixth the Americans breached this line, and the Germans shortened their front to avoid encirclement in the salient. Dettling wrote:

> Until then the fighting was extraordinarily hard, with many losses. The units had, with very few exceptions, conducted themselves superbly. Often battle groups including battalion staffs were outflanked and surrounded in carrying out their defensive tasks, only to be freed in a counterattack or else to fight their own way out.... The fighting strength of the battalions averaged approximately 120 to 130 men [barely enough for a company].

The Germans' counterattack broke up their own line, as von Kluge had feared, offering the Allies the chance of a great pincer movement from north and south, which Montgomery hoped would encircle what was left of the 7th Army and Panzer Group West.

(Opposite) As a tank burns in the distance, Canadian soldiers advance along the road from Caen to Falaise. (Right) After breaking out of Normandy, the Americans swung east toward Argentan. The Canadians and Poles raced down the Caen-Falaise Road in what was called Operation Totalize. (Below) Canadian tanks mobilize for their role in Totalize. (Bottom) A Canadian truck burns after American aircraft attacked it by mistake — an unfortunate, and not always avoidable, side effect of the "fog of war."

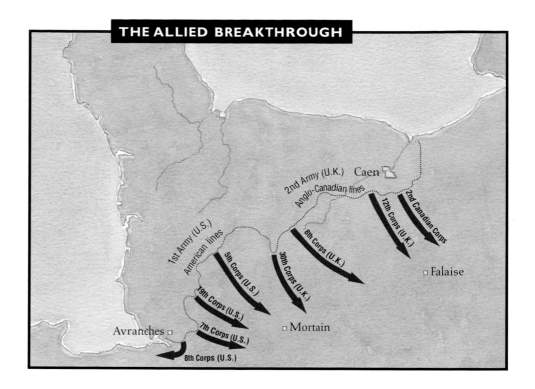

THE ALLIED BREAKTHROUGH

Operation Totalize on August 8 set the 1st Canadian Army in motion from the north toward Falaise, a town twenty miles due south of Caen and fourteen north of Argentan. Bradley, meanwhile, after consulting Eisenhower and Montgomery, ordered the XV Corps from Patton's 3rd Army to move toward Argentan from the west and south to spring the trap on the Germans.

THREE DAYS EARLIER, MONTGOMERY HAD FINALLY LOST PATIENCE WITH THE LAGGARDLY GENERALS of the XXX Corps. He fired its commander, Bucknall, and also Erskine of the consistently underachieving 7th Armoured Division. The energetic Lieutenant General Sir Brian Horrocks took over the corps, which seemed to acquire a new esprit overnight. As his VIII Corps ran down the flank of the German 7th Army, General O'Connor was able to send the 11th Armoured Division into the gap between that army and Panzer Group West. But Montgomery diverted him away from the town of Vire, undefended at the time, because it was in the American sector. At the same time, however, he agreed to let the Americans into the British sector at Argentan.

Two infantry divisions from the II Canadian Corps (Lieutenant General G. G. Simonds) moved off on August 8 after a huge bomber attack but no preliminary artillery barrage. Behind them, ready to exploit any gap punched into the German line, were the 4th Canadian Armoured Division and 1st Polish Armored Division (Major General Stanislaw Maczek). Both tank formations were fresh to the campaign and inexperienced. General Simonds now produced Canada's contribution to the array of "funny" tanks in

Normandy — the "Kangaroo." Converted from the tank-like chassis of a "Priest" self-propelled gun, it was defrocked of its 25-pounder cannon and given a thick steel roof — the armored personnel carrier. Seventy-six were adapted in three days for Totalize, in which the Canadians and Poles were supported by the British 51st Highland Division and their 33rd Armoured Brigade.

Phase one, a drive by armor and infantry to force a break in the German line, went well. Phase two, an armored thrust by Canadian, Polish and British tanks through the gap, was less successful. The usual traffic jams built up amid confusion compounded by serious errors on the part of American aircraft — which all too often bombed their own side. All this gave General Meyer the time and opportunity to bring up elements of his residual 12th SS Panzer Division to oppose the planned thrust of the Polish and Canadian armored divisions toward Falaise.

The Canadians took on any German strongpoint they came across instead of bypassing it, which slowed them down even further. Meanwhile, the XV U.S. Corps with the 79th and 90th Infantry Divisions, backed by the 5th U.S. Armored Division and the 2nd French Armored Division (commanded by Général de division Jacques Philippe Leclerc, nom de guerre of the dashing Philippe Marie, Vicomte de Hautecloque), advanced toward Argentan, where Bradley temporarily called a halt. The Canadians finally captured Falaise on August 16 — too late to close the gap between themselves and the Americans to their south at that point. The Germans were therefore still moving east in their attempt to evade the not-quite-closed pincers.

The gap was now about fifteen miles wide, and the bulk of the surviving German forces in northwest France was concentrated in the "Falaise Pocket." The only way out to the east was the "Falaise

The Price Canada Paid for Victory

Many Canadians feel that their country is still denied due credit for its contribution during the Second World War. Physically vast but demographically small, Canada was overshadowed by America and Britain and was viewed as a glorified breadbasket with no real role in the making of history. In fact, Canada made a significant contribution to victory in Europe, paying an enormous human price — as well as a domestic and political one.

Of the thirty-nine divisions involved in Operation Overlord, three were Canadian. The Americans contributed twenty; the British, fourteen; and France and Poland, one each. Of the roughly 1.93 million troops engaged, some 100,000 were Canadians — 5.2 percent. And every Canadian overseas was a volunteer. On July 23, 1944, the three Canadian divisions (together with the Poles' 1st Armored Division and a Canadian tank brigade) formed the separate 1st Canadian Army — this, from a country whose standing army had numbered just 4,000 in 1939.

Proportionately, Canadian battle casualties were very high. Of a total of 192,000 killed, wounded, missing or captured under British command, 42,000 (twenty-two percent) were Canadian. Of the 41,500 killed, 9,900 (twenty-one percent) were Canadian. Indeed, the 3rd Canadian Division was unsurpassed for casualties in Montgomery's Army Group between D-Day and the end of the war in Europe; the 2nd was only slightly less damaged.

By fall 1944, the Canadian army faced a severe manpower shortage. Conscription had been introduced in 1940, but only for home service. The topic was one that split the country along language lines — with English Canadians in favor, and French Canadians against. The government hemmed and hawed, then finally starting sending conscripts overseas — a move that cost them support in Quebec, led to some unrest there and further poisoned relations between French- and English-speaking Canadians.

Come on CANADA!

Gap." The fighting there was exceptionally harsh, despite the almost complete disarray of the Germans. Both sides in this climactic and convoluted battle agreed that the devastation was exceptionally ghastly. General Dettling wrote:

> The scene in the pocket was shattering. Roads were stuffed with shot-up horses, carts and motor vehicles of all kinds, with groups of the most varied divisions and formations in the fields. There were heavy artillery barrages the whole day through, [aimed] almost concentrically on villages, paths, copses, hedgerows and cart tracks, not to mention [closely] observed fire on movements of all sorts.

Company Sergeant Major Symes of the 5th/7th Hampshires, fighting with the Canadians, remembered:

> We went into the Falaise Gap at Chambois…and [saw] absolute carnage.… One of the big surprises to us was that there were several elderly French ladies that were going through the pockets of the dead Germans, climbing up into the back of vehicles and taking things. So dead bodies didn't seem to mean anything to these French ladies at all. They were taking wallets from the German dead, rings off their fingers, whatever they could get their hands on.

Lieutenant Cyril Brain, recruited in a London club to be a "phantom officer" (gathering battlefield intelligence), was attached to the Polish division, one of the formations chosen with Canadian and Free French troops to close the gap by moving south toward the oncoming Americans:

> The Germans fought doggedly and efficiently to try and stop us closing…the gap at Falaise because this was the way back to Germany if they had to withdraw.… We were to be supported by the RAF.… The first wave passed over us and dropped its bombs where the Germans were, in the middle of a wood facing us, but the second wave unloaded their bombs upon us. This was another terrible mistake.… The Poles and the Canadians again took a pasting and some two hundred were wounded — and about 150 lost their lives.… I was with General Maczek and the Polish command vehicle, which he always took as far forward as he possibly could, and I could see with my binoculars the Germans trying to get out from Normandy up this narrow valley.… The Americans under General Patton were coming up from the south to try and close the gap. They were a bit enthusiastic from time to time and we received a number of their shells. It was, let's face it, a bit of a shambles.

So bad was the stench of death that even fighter pilots could smell it as they swiftly flew over the battlefield.

Flying into the Falaise Gap

Already a seasoned U.S. combat fighter pilot at twenty-two, Quentin Aanenson (above) miraculously survived a number of harrowing missions, including the one at Falaise:

"The fighter-bombers of the 9th Air Force were assigned to protect Patton's right flank from German counterattacks, clear the roads ahead of him, do as much killing of Germans in front of him as we could.… We were trying to close the door before the German forces could be withdrawn. It became known as the battle for the Falaise Pocket — but for us it was a killing ground. We caught and killed German troops in large numbers. We destroyed so much equipment on the ground that roads and fields were literally covered with burning or burnt-out vehicles. Bodies could be seen everywhere.… But we took our licks, too, and I lost more of my buddies."

Holding the Hill at Falaise

Paul Koczula (below) was with the 1st Polish Armored Division during the battle for the Falaise Pocket. The division had been dispatched to France in late July 1944 to operate as part of the 1st Canadian Corps. On August 25, the Poles seized Hill 262 (nicknamed the Mace, for its shape) and dug in their tanks on the heights. Low on fuel and surrounded on both sides by German units frantic to escape before the Falaise Gap closed, the Poles put up a heroic fight in the face of overwhelming odds. As one of the tank mechanics, Paul Koczula had to brave enemy fire repeatedly in the front lines to service the armored vehicles and other equipment.

THE POLES FROM THE NORTH AND THE AMERICAN 90TH INFANTRY DIVISION FROM THE SOUTH joined hands and closed the Gap twelve miles southeast of Falaise at the villages of Trun and Chambois. The remnants of some ten German divisions might have been hopelessly surrounded in the Pocket but there was one last, fierce engagement in which the Germans managed briefly to turn the tables. They surrounded one element of their many enemies — the 1st Polish Armored Division, ensconced on Hill 262, which came under simultaneous attack from German units inside and outside the Pocket as the Gap was closing. Waffen SS Officer Otto Weidinger recalled:

> [The Poles] felt enclosed themselves and fought at Hill 262 and Boisjois as if on an island in the stream of German forces surging against them from both sides. Their losses, sixteen officers and 335 other ranks, were therefore correspondingly high. The German attack from the east was a complete surprise for the Poles.

Hubert Meyer described how his namesake, Major General Kurt "Panzer" Meyer of the 12th SS Panzer "Hitler Youth" Division, managed to break out of the Falaise Pocket as the Gap closed:

> On the morning of August 20 the encirclement was not quite complete to the east. Between the position of a battle group of the 1st Polish Armored Division…on Hill 262 and the foremost positions of the 2nd French Armored Division northeast of Chambois, there was no firm strongpoint or closed barrier. The land in between was overlooked [from the north], more or less effectively, by Poles, Canadians and French, who often exchanged their positions…. Thanks to the attack by a battle group from the 2nd SS "Das Reich" Division…from outside, the Pocket was opened so wide that many larger and smaller groups with vehicles or on foot were able to break out of encirclement…. Some divisions…were able to escape encirclement in whole or in part. Through simultaneous attacks from without and within, notable forces succeeded in breaking out of the Pocket. No formations, but only groups of remnants of various units, capitulated.

This is a somewhat rosy view of the end of the Normandy campaign — the greatest defeat the German army suffered in the Second World War, greater even than Stalingrad. Some ten thousand Germans were killed in the Falaise Pocket alone and about fifty thousand were taken prisoner; perhaps twenty thousand escaped eastward to cross the Seine in a remarkably orderly retreat. Before that, however, some forty German divisions had been knocked out, if not destroyed. About two hundred thousand men had been killed or wounded and a similar number captured in the campaign as a whole.

Fleeing through the Falaise Gap

German paratrooper Gerhard R. Käppner (right), managed to get out of Normandy before the Allies closed the Falaise Gap:

(Above) German prisoners captured at Falaise are loaded onto trucks for transportation to POW camps. (Right) Gerhard Käppner's army identification.

"We couldn't take any of our equipment…. We just streamed back with our small arms, and we re-assembled somewhere near the Seine…. Well, the orders were that we make a stand in the daytime. If we were attacked we fight back. If we weren't attacked we just kept quiet and moved out during the night…. We got back as far as Belgium…. It was very hot…and we were too lazy to put on our helmets…. By surprise, we got caught by mortar fire which we didn't expect, and something hit me on the head and some on the face, and that was the end of the war for me."

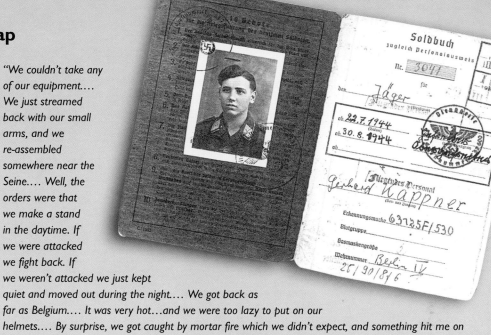

On August 19 the advance guard of Patton's 3rd Army reached the Seine; the 79th U.S. Division was the first to cross it that night. Eisenhower tactfully diverted Leclerc's division from Falaise to drive to Paris so that Frenchmen were able to liberate their own capital on August 25.

IN ROUND FIGURES, THE UNITED STATES ARMY ENDURED 126,000 casualties (sixty percent of the total): 21,000 killed, 95,000 wounded, 10,000 missing. The British and Canadian armies took 83,000 casualties (forty percent, including Poles): 16,000 killed, 58,000 wounded, 9,000 missing. Twenty American divisions (perhaps 1.2 million men, or sixty-three percent of the total) took part in D-Day and its aftermath, compared with fourteen British, three Canadian and one Polish (possibly 720,000 men in all, thirty-seven percent). Proportionately, therefore, Anglo-Canadian casualties were slightly higher than American — though lower in sheer numbers.

The USAAF had 8,500 casualties; the RAF's numbered 8,200. Nobody knows precisely how many air force casualties were incurred in Overlord-related prior operations but they probably ran well into five figures. Naval losses were numbered in hundreds.

GENERAL SIR BERNARD MONTGOMERY, COMMANDER IN CHIEF OF THE Allied armies that invaded Normandy, came under fierce attack from American commanders, U.S. politicians and the media — and even his own government — during a most difficult campaign against a powerful and resourceful enemy. As high command requires, he was ultimately responsible for the mistakes, pulled punches, delays and opportunities missed by the troops on the ground. By the same token, he deserved (and never hesitated to claim!) the credit for what was ultimately an overwhelming success. He therefore has the last word:

I reckoned we would be on the general line of the Seine within three months, that would be by D+90.

Patton got there on D+75; Paris fell on D+80. On September 1, as Eisenhower crossed over from England to take personal charge of the Allied forces for the march on Germany, Montgomery was promoted to field marshal. In summarizing the campaign for the BBC, the incorrigible self-promoter could not resist adding, triumphantly, if not quite truthfully:

It was all exactly as planned.

The Beginning of the End

"Crushing and complete victory over the German enemy has been secured."
— Lieutenant General Henry D. G. Crerar, in a message to all ranks of the 1st Canadian Army, May 4, 1945

MONTGOMERY'S PREVIOUS victory at the battle of El Alamein in autumn 1942 was described by Churchill as "not the beginning of the end, but the end of the beginning." The victory in Normandy, however, was undoubtedly the beginning of the end of the war in Europe.

But the defeat of Nazi Germany could still hardly be taken for granted. As the Red Army continued to engage the bulk of the Wehrmacht, the Western Allies pressed northeastward toward Germany's industrial heart, the Ruhr, via the Low Countries. Other American and French forces, landed in the south of France in Operation Dragoon on August 15, drove northward toward Austria and Germany. Yet Anglo-American forces in Italy, reduced for Dragoon, still had an uphill struggle to beat back the Germans in the north — who would fight on for eight more months.

The Germans had also just deployed the world's first cruise missile — the V1 — against London and the port of Antwerp. The world's first ballistic missile — the V2 — soon followed. Germany was racing to produce revolutionary submarines capable of evading nearly all contemporary convoy escorts. Only the Allied air campaign staved off this new threat to the Allied transatlantic supply line by bombing the relevant shipyards and factories. The Luftwaffe had deployed in significant numbers the world's first operational jet, the Messerschmitt Me 262. It was only Hitler's stupidity in insisting it be adapted for bombing that prevented it from decimating the Allied strategic air forces.

General Dettling described how his 363rd Infantry Division spent its last days in Normandy. On the night of August 20, he wrote, the division was divided into groups to break out of the Falaise Pocket. All their heavier weapons were lost, along with most of their horses, carts and motor vehicles. About two thousand men were left, and some five hundred stragglers eventually joined them — raising the residue to a quarter of the original strength. Nevertheless, these exhausted, beaten soldiers assembled as ordered at the village of Le Sap, less than twenty miles east of the closed Gap, for a few hours' rest on August 21:

> On the same day the order arrived from Army that the division, along with a few others, was to be reconstituted in the Reich...at Wildflecken in the Röhn [area of Bavaria].

So this "broken" formation reached Cambrai in northern France by a series of forced night marches of thirty to forty kilometers each — and caught the last train to Wildflecken on September 4!

Two weeks later there was much starker proof that it was too early to write off the German army. Montgomery tried a thrust against the Ruhr by attempting to seize the Rhine bridge at Arnhem in the southeast Netherlands, using British and American paratroopers. The British 1st Airborne Division was roundly defeated by two German armored divisions regrouping there after Normandy and was reduced to about the same size as the rump of the 363rd.

Three months later the Germans were still capable of a last offensive in the Ardennes that achieved total surprise, forced a "bulge" in the American line and almost broke through. This became the U.S. Army's largest land battle of the entire war (the Battle of the Bulge) and once again engaged the well-traveled 101st Airborne Division — which was relieved after an epic, eight-day stand at Bastogne thanks largely to a spectacular, high-speed advance by Patton's tanks.

The eastern and western fronts against Germany met at Torgau on the river Elbe on April 27, 1945, when American and Soviet troops joined hands. By that time the British army had liberated (and filmed) the concentration camp at Bergen-Belsen in northwest Germany — a gruesome reminder of why the war against Hitler had been fought.

On May 4, at Lüneberg Heath, Montgomery accepted the surrender of German forces in northwest Germany, Holland and Denmark. On May 7, at Rheims in northern France, Eisenhower's chief of staff, General Smith, along with Russian and French representatives, negotiated the surrender of all German forces. Hostilities were to end at midnight on May 8. Japan held out until the first atomic bombs forced its capitulation in August 1945.

On May 8, 1945, troops of the Canadian army, having entered North Holland, marched into my hometown of Alkmaar, where they gave me a ride on a tank and a very large biscuit — the like of which I had never seen before.

For them it was the end of a long march that had begun for the Allied armies eleven months before at Juno and the other beaches in Normandy on the morning of June 6, 1944. For my family and me, and for millions of Western Europeans, it was freedom — the gift of life itself.

(Above) The author as a young boy joins a British soldier on guard duty in the town of Alkmaar, Holland, shortly after its liberation in May 1945. (Bottom left) Lest we forget. La Cambe is the largest of the six German military cemeteries in Normandy. It holds 21,115 of the 77,936 German soldiers buried in this area of France. (Bottom right) The American Normandy Cemetery at Coleville-sur-Mer, not far from Omaha Beach, contains 9,386 graves.

BIBLIOGRAPHY

Ambrose, Stephen. *D-Day, June 6 1944: The Climactic Battle of World War II*. New York: Simon & Schuster, 1994.

Arnold-Forster, Mark. *The World at War*. London: Pimlico, 2001.

Boberach, Heinz. *Meldungen aus dem Reich* (Messages from the Reich). Neuwied/Berlin: Luchterhand, 1965.

Chalmers, Rear Admiral W. S. *Full Cycle: The Biography of Admiral Sir Bertram Home Ramsay*. London: Hodder & Stoughton, 1959.

D'Este, Carlo. *Decision in Normandy*. London: Penguin, 2001.

Desquesnes, Rèmy. *Normandy 1944*. Trans. John Lee. Rennes, France: Editions Ouest-France/Memorial de Caen, 1993.

Dixon, Norman F. *On the Psychology of Military Incompetence*. London: Pimlico, 1994.

Eisenhower, Dwight D. *Crusade in Europe*. London: Heinemann, 1948.

Eisenhower, Dwight D. *D-Day to VE-Day: Report to U.S. Senate and U.K. Parliament*. London: Stationery Office, 2000.

Foot, M. R. D. *S.O.E: The Special Operations Executive, 1940–1946*. London: Pimlico, 1999.

Granatstein, J. L., and Desmond Morton. *Bloody Victory: Canadians and the D-Day Campaign, 1944*. Toronto: Lester Publishing, 1994.

Hastings, Max. *Overlord*. London: Pan Books, 1999.

Haswell, Jock. *The Intelligence and Deception of the D-Day Landings*. London: Batsford, 1979.

Hinsley, F. H., and C. A. G. Simkins. *British Intelligence in the Second World War*. Vol. 4, *Security & Counter-Intelligence*. London: HMSO, 1990.

Howard, Michael. *British Intelligence in the Second World War*. Vol. 5, *Strategic Deception*. London: HMSO, 1990.

Isby, David C., ed. *Fighting the Invasion: The German Army at D-Day*. London: Greenhill Books, 2000.

Jary, Sydney. *18 Platoon*. Surrey, England: Sydney Jary, 1987.

Keegan, John. *Six Armies in Normandy*. London: Pimlico, 1992.

Kershaw, Ian. *Hitler 1936–1945: Nemesis*. London: Penguin, 2001.

Kimball, Warren F., ed. *Churchill and Roosevelt: The Complete Correspondence*. 3 vols. Princeton, NJ: Princeton University Press, 1984.

Larrabee, Eric. *Commander in Chief*. New York: Harper & Row, 1987.

Miller, Russell. *Nothing Less than Victory: The Oral History of D-Day*. New York: William Morrow, 1998.

Morgan, Ted. *FDR: A Biography*. London: Grafton, 1987.

Neillands, Robin, and Roderick De Normann. *D-Day 1944: Voices from Normandy*. London: Cassell, 2001.

Oberkommando der Wehrmacht. *Die Wehrmachtberichte 1939–1945* (Wehrmacht daily reports 1939–1945). 3 vols. Cologne: Gesellschaft für Literatur und Bildung, 1989.

Royal Navy Historical Branch. *Operation "Neptune": Landings in Normandy, June 1944.* London: HMSO, 1994.

Ruge, Friedrich. *Rommel in der Normandie.* Stuttgart: K. F. Kochler Verlag, 1959.

Ryan, Cornelius. *The Longest Day: June 6, 1944.* New York: Simon & Schuster, 1959.

Smith, Claude. *The History of the Glider Pilot Regiment.* London: Leo Cooper, 1992.

Speidel, Hans. *Invasion 1944: Ein Beitrag zu Rommels und des Reiches Schicksal* (A contribution to the fate of Rommel and the Reich). Stuttgart: H. Lemis, Tübingen, 1949.

Stacey, C. P. *The Victory Campaign: The Operations in Northwest Europe, 1944–1945.* Ottawa: Queen's Printer, 1966.

Stagg, J. N. *Forecast for Overlord.* London: Ian Allan, 1971.

Van der Vat, Dan. *The Good Nazi: The Life and Lies of Albert Speer.* London: George Weidenfeld & Nicholson, 1997.

Van der Vat, Dan. *Standard of Power: The Royal Navy in the Twentieth Century.* London: Hutchinson, 2000.

TELL YOUR STORY

Several organizations dedicate themselves to preserving the memories of veterans of the Second World War. If you have a story to tell, or know someone who does, you might consider contacting the following:

CANADA

The Dominion Institute has created The Memory Project, which, among other things, collects veterans' reminiscences:
www.thememoryproject.com

UNITED KINGDOM

The D-Day and Normandy Fellowship collects veterans' first-person accounts:
www.eurosurf.com/DDNF

The Second World War Experience Centre gathers accounts and objects connected largely, but not exclusively, to the British experience in World War II:
www.war-experience.org

UNITED STATES

The University of New Orleans' Eisenhower Center for American Studies has an oral history project focusing on Normandy and the Battle of the Bulge:
www.uno.edu/~eice/oralhistory.htm

The George C. Marshall Foundation Memories Project:
www.marshallfoundation.org/educational/memories_project.htm

The American Folklife Center at the Library of Congress runs the Veterans History Project for veterans of all American wars:
www.loc.gov/folklife/vets

CHAPTER EIGHT
108–109: NARA.
110–111: IWM B5111.
111: (Inset left) IWM MH24291. (Inset right) IWM B5114.
112: (Top and middle) TM. (Bottom) Courtesy of Ken Oakley.
113: (Top) IWM B5063. (Middle) TM. (Bottom) IWM MH2012.
114: (Top left and right) TM. (Bottom left) G.C.A. Gilbert/SWWEC.
115: (Inset) IWM B5041.
116: NAC PA-132790.
117: (Left) NAC PA-132651. (Right) Courtesy of Gary Pawson.
118: (Left) Courtesy of Stanley Seneco. (Right) QORC.
119: (Inset) IWM FLM3566.
120: QORC.
121: CWM (Except inset middle).
122: CWM.
123: (Left) Courtesy of James B. Prendergast. (Right) NAC PA-132895.
124: (Inset left) NAC PA-132384. (Inset right) NAC PA-136280.

125: (Inset) Courtesy of William McCormick.
126: (Inset) TM.
127: (Top) IWM MH2014. (Bottom) Courtesy of Charles Eagles.
128: (Bottom) Courtesy of John P. Cummer.
128–129: Courtesy of Charles Eagles.
130: (Left) Courtesy of Paul Cheall. (Right) TM.
131: (Top left) HA. Newspaper courtesy of Gary Pawson. (Bottom) Courtesy of Jean Deshane.
132: (Inset) TM.
133: (Top) IWM BU1036. (Inset, bottom left) IWM B5696.

CHAPTER NINE
134–135: TM.
135: (Inset) BA.
137: (Top) BA. (Bottom) TM.
138: (Inset) IWM A24511.
140: (Top) HA. (Bottom) Courtesy of William K. Newell.
141: (Left) Courtesy of Bill Davison. (Right) Courtesy of William K. Newell.

142: (Insets, left and right) NARA. (Inset, middle) Courtesy of Al Castillo.
143: BA.
144: Courtesy of Leslie Dinning.
145: IWM CL672.
146: (Left) NHC. (Right) NARA.
147: IWM B6000. (Inset) IWM B6017.
148: L. David Brook/Pen & Sword Books Ltd.
149: Courtesy of Sydney Jary.
150: (Top) IWM CL347. (Bottom) NAC PA-116516.
151: CWM.
152: Ken Davenport/SWWEC.
153: Hulton-Deutsch Collection/C/M. (Inset left) IWM B6799. (Inset middle and inset right) Bettmann/C/M.

CHAPTER TEN
154: AKG London.
155: BA.
156: (Inset) Hulton-Deutsch Collection/C/M.
157: (Top) NARA. (Bottom) Courtesy of Sally Slingluff.

158: (Top) NARA. (Middle) Dwight Shepler/NHC. (Bottom) C/M.
160: (Top) NAC PA-162435. (Middle) NARA. (Bottom) Bettmann/C/M.
161: (Left) Courtesy of Frank W. Towers. (Right) AKG London.

CHAPTER ELEVEN
162: NARA.
164: NAC PA-131375.
165: (Top left) NAC PA-132904. (Bottom left) NAC PA-132657.
166: Canadian War Poster Collection, Rare Books and Special Collections Division, McGill University Libraries.
167: Courtesy of Quentin Aanenson.
168: Courtesy of Paul Koczula.
169: (Left) Hulton-Deutsch Collection/C/M. (Right) Gerhard R. Käppner/SWWEC.

EPILOGUE
171: (Top) Courtesy of Dan van der Vat.

ACKNOWLEDGMENTS

■ I should like to thank the following for their help with the preparation of this book: Michael Shaw (for the last time as my literary agent, now retired) and Jonathan Pegg at Curtis Brown Ltd.; Ian Coutts, Hugh Brewster and the staff at Madison Press Books; Lieutenant-Colonel Andrew Pinion of Holts Battlefield Tours; and Lieutenant-Colonel Lawrie Phillips.

I am no less grateful to the staffs of the following institutions: Imperial War Museum, London (especially the Sound Archive) and Duxford; Airborne Forces Museum, Aldershot; D-Day Museum, Southsea; Federal German Military Archive (Bundesarchiv-Militärarchiv), Freiburg; London Library; Richmond upon Thames Libraries (especially the Twickenham branch).

— *Dan van der Vat*

■ Madison Press Books would like to thank the following individuals for their invaluable help during the course of this project: David Fletcher, curator of The Tank Museum; Edward Lapotsky, director and historian of the C-47 Club and coordinator of the World War II Society Europe; John McCabe at the University of Ohio; director William McIntosh and director of research and archives Carol Tuckwiller, both of the National D-Day Memorial Foundation; Ray Tapio of Critical Hit Inc.; and Paula Ussery, curator of collections at the National D-Day Museum. In addition, we are indebted to Emily Ferguson for her dogged photo research in England.

Special thanks are due to the following people who helped us get in touch with veterans and some of whom also provided valuable information and memorabilia: L. David Brook, editor of *The Eagle*, the journal of the Glider Pilot Regimental Association; Eddie Clark, webmaster of www.dday.co.uk; Patrick Elie, webmaster of www.6juin1944.com; Arlette Gondrée Pritchett; and Peter Simundson of the Queen's Own Rifles of Canada Regimental Museum. Particular thanks to Peter Liddle and the Second World War Experience Centre in Horsforth, Leeds, England. The Centre, a repository of stories and memorabilia connected to the war, provided the photographs and first-person accounts for Sadie Greaves, G. A. C. Gilbert, Ken Davenport and Gerhard R. Käppner used in this book.

We are grateful to John S. D. Eisenhower and J. L. Granatstein for their consultation work and the Introductions they wrote for the various editions of this book. Thanks also to Peter Liddle of the Second World War Experience Centre for his expert consultation.

Editorial Director: Hugh M. Brewster
Associate Editorial Director: Wanda Nowakowska
Project Editor: Ian R. Coutts
Editor/Eyewitness Accounts: Catherine Fraccaro
Editorial Assistance: Imoinda Romain
Art Director: Gordon Sibley
Graphic Designer: Jennifer Lum
Production Director: Susan Barrable
Production Manager: Donna Chong
Color Separation: Colour Technologies
Printing and Binding: Oceanic Graphic Printing, China

D-Day: The Greatest Invasion — A People's History was produced by Madison Press Books, which is under the direction of Albert E. Cummings.

QUOTATION CREDITS

Wartime broadcasts, from the BBC, London.

All German quotations (translated by the author) derive from recordings in the Federal German Military Archive (Bundesarchiv-Militärarchiv), except for the opening passage of Chapter Nine, which is from *Meldungen aus dem Reich* (see Bibliography).

Eugene E. Eckstam, from the Oral Histories of the U.S. Naval Historical Center, Washington, DC (1994).

Dwight D. Eisenhower, from *Crusade in Europe* and from *D-Day to V-E Day* (see Bibliography).

Bertram Ramsay, from his wartime diary in the Naval Archive at Churchill College, Cambridge.

James Stagg, from *Forecast for Overlord* (see Bibliography).

James West Thompson, from the Oral Histories of the U.S. Naval Historical Center, Washington, DC (2001).

The following quotations are from interviews conducted and/or preserved by the Imperial War Museum Sound Archive:

Ramsay Bader (10593/3, 1989)
Philip Branson (13266/4, 1993)
Peter Brown (13854/3, 1994)
Doon Campbell (17036/C/A, 1984)
Rolland Duff (14824/1 and 2, 1994)
Simone Duncomb (17012/C/C, 1984)
William French (13144/2 and 3, 1993)
Norman Habetin (10385/3 and 4, 1993)
Geoffrey Hayward (17014, 1984)
Jean Houel (17038/C/C, 1984)
Ron Howard (16731/4, 1992)
Roland Johnston (14109/0, 1988)

R. V. Jones (16987/B/A, 1984)
Edward Kendall (13150/4, 1993)
Derek Knight (17020/D/B, 1984)
Lord Lovat (17035, 1984)
Donald May (13762/2, 1994)
William Millin (11614/2 and 3, 1990)
Ronald Mole (13420/3, 1993)
Bernard Montgomery (12002, 1959)
John Phillips (16978, 1984)
Richard Todd (17059/E/D, 1984)
Arthur Wildman (9139/1 and 3, 1985)
Red Wright (17015/B/A, 1984)